D1047543

THE DEFENDER'S GUIDE FOR LIFE'S TOUGHEST QUESTIONS

**Preparing Today's Believers for the
Onslaught of Secular Humanism**

{ Ray Comfort }

First printing: January 2011

Master Books®, P.O. Box 726, Green Forest, AR 72638
Master Books is a division of New Leaf Publishing Group, Inc.

ISBN: 978-0-89051-604-1
Library of Congress Number: 2010943232

Cover by Heidi Rohr Design
Interior design by Diana Bogardus

Please consider requesting that a copy of this volume be purchased by your local library system.

Printed in the United States of America

Please visit our website for other great titles:
www.masterbooks.net

For information regarding author interviews,
please contact the publicity department at (870) 438-5288

Master
Books®
A Division of New Leaf Publishing Group
www.masterbooks.net

Contents

Preface

There is a popular atheist poster that says, "Atheism: Good enough for these idiots." The "idiots" pictured in the poster are icons of history — from top left there are the faces of Ernest Hemingway, Abraham Lincoln, Carl Sagan, Mark Twain, Thomas Jefferson, Benjamin Franklin, Albert Einstein, and of course, Charles Darwin.

This poster is typical of those who called themselves atheists. For example, Thomas Jefferson said, "I have ever thought religion a concern purely between our God and our consciences, for which we were accountable to Him, and not to the priests."[1] He wasn't an atheist. Albert Einstein lamented the fact that atheists lied about his beliefs: "In view of such harmony in the cosmos which I, with my limited human mind, am able to recognize, there are yet people who say there is no God. But what makes me really angry is that they quote me for support of such views."[2] The brilliant and witty Mark Twain despised organized religion, but he wasn't an atheist. He said, "None of us can be as great as God, but any of us can be as good."[3] Benjamin Franklin loved the God who gave him life — "It is that particular wise and good God, who is the author and owner of our system, that I propose for the object of my praise and adoration."[4] Charles Darwin was disillusioned with Christianity, but he was far from being an atheist. He said, "When thus reflecting I feel compelled to look to a First Cause having an intelligent mind in some degree analogous to that of man; and I deserve to be called a Theist."[5] President Abraham Lincoln revered God, and said, "While we are grateful to all the brave men and officers for the events of the past few days, we should, above all, be very grateful to Almighty God, who gives us victory."[6] The famous American astronomer and author Carl Sagan, who went to meet his Maker, dying of cancer in December 1996, was also not an atheist. He said, "An agnostic is somebody who doesn't believe in something until there is evidence for it, so I'm agnostic."[7] Carl Sagan didn't know if God existed.

There is one atheist in the poster — Ernest Hemingway. He was the American author who wrote fiction and made the profound statement, "All thinking men are atheists." He is said to be "a hero to atheists everywhere." Sadly, he was an alcoholic who became so depressed with life he "put the end of the barrel into his mouth, pulled the trigger, and blew out his brains."[8] On seeing the poster, one atheist said, "Ugh, I don't think Hemingway is a good advertisement for atheism due to his alcoholism and suicide.[9] Surely we could find people with lives that ended happier than his for this poster?"[10] Another remarked, "If you sat down and really talked with those guys, I'm sure they'd all admit to 'atheism' in restricted senses of the word, though."[11] Sure.

So there you have it. The one poster boy for atheism is a pretty pathetic advertisement. And you can't blame Hemingway for killing himself. He had no idea where he came from, what he was doing on earth, or where he was going when death eventually came. All atheists are *unthinking* men, but when it comes down to it there really aren't too many of them. As Sir Isaac Newton so wisely said, "Atheism is so senseless and odious to mankind that it never had many professors."[12]

Chapter One

Humanity: Rights and Suffering

Why do you concentrate on Darwin's alleged racism but mysteriously fall silent about your own religion's support and outright endorsement of the filthy practice of slavery? You're a complete hypocrite, Ray.

Both thy bondmen, and thy bondmaids, which thou shalt have, shall be of the heathen that are round about you; of them shall ye buy bondmen and bondmaids. Moreover of the children of the strangers that do sojourn among you, of them shall ye buy, and of their families that are with you, which they begat in your land: and they shall be your possession. And ye shall take them as an inheritance for your children after you, to inherit them for a possession; they shall be your bondmen for ever: but over your brethren the children of Israel, ye shall not rule one over another with rigour (Leviticus 25:44–46; KJV).

There is no denying it — the Bible not only condones slavery, it encourages it, tells owners how to treat their slaves, and even instructs owners on what they are to do if their slave needs punishment.

Before you slam this book closed and claim a slam dunk against the Bible, it's important for you to realize that we look at the issue through the colored glasses of cruel slavery of the American South. We think of slaves as being rounded up like wild animals, packed into ships, held in chains, starved to the point of death, cruelly whipped, sold like chattel, and treated worse than dogs. History shapes the word "slave" that way for us.

However, in most cases the word "slave" in Scripture and the word "servant" are interchangeable. Replace the word "slave" with the word "servant" and it will help to bring the issue into perspective for you. If you study biblical admonitions to slaves, when they were set free, they were given the option to stay as slaves for life, if they so desired.

I said "most cases" because people sold themselves into slavery when they were in debt. There were slaves taken in war. The Jews were taken and used as slaves when they were in Egypt, and they were treated with terrible cruelty.

It is important to realize that both the Old and New Testaments condemn the practice of what it calls "man-stealing." This is what happened in Africa in the 19th century. Innocent Africans were cruelly kidnapped from their loved ones by slave-hunters, who sold them to slave-traders, who brought them to the United Sates to work on plantations and farms. This practice is so condemned by God that the penalty for such a crime in the Mosaic Law was death: "Anyone who kidnaps another and either sells him or still has him when he is caught must be put to death" (Exodus 21:16; NIV).

Sadly, much of American slavery was "justified" from Bible verses. But that is nothing new. Throughout history men have twisted the Bible for their own selfish gain. Hitler did it to foster hatred for the Jews, when he painted them as "Christ-killers." What this does is confirm the biblical truth that the human heart truly is wicked (including mine).

Like most other members of my species, I sometimes find life overwhelming and absurd. I struggle with the knowledge that the people I love will eventually die, and that their deaths will almost certainly be preceded by a period of suffering and decline. More selfishly, I am conscious of my own numbered days, my own vulnerability to sickness and decay.

Any thinking person who looks at this life with all of its pains and struggles is going to feel "overwhelmed." Millions try to find refuge in drugs or in alcohol. Most try to deal with their dread of death by using the word "eventually," thinking that they are putting it off into the distant future. But the reality is, millions are cut off by death in their youth and they find that their "eventually" wasn't distant at all.

When I was 20 years old, I began thinking for the first time in my godless life. I thought about life's purpose and its fragility, and how it seemed insane that we had the amazing ability to put a man on the moon, and yet we didn't even know what we were doing here on earth. I thought it strange that medical science spent billions of dollars trying to find a cure for the common cold, and it did nothing to try to stop the aging process. It seemed insane that we were all going to die and nobody talked about it, asked why, or even looked for an answer to it.

So I thought that it was wise to simply live a long, healthy life. I would try to die healthy. I decided to visit my doctor to see if he had some advice. Hope dissipated as I watched him light up a cigarette and breathe the carcinogen-filled smoke into his sick-looking body.

Neither can a fantasy help, one that tells us we are nothing but part of a "species." Then again, each of us can, at any moment in time, stop believing the fantasy and with a little thought use our God-given eyes and ears to know that God exists. This amazing place we call a "universe" didn't happen by accident.

Each of us (by the grace of God) can listen to the voice of our conscience, know that we have sinned against His perfect law, and understand that Hell is a reality. It's then that the Cross will make sense. Upon our repentance and faith in Jesus, God will give us everlasting life and lift us out of the futility of a godless lifestyle.

You should stop using the criminal justice system as an analogy for your God. As you have had pointed out many times, it is entirely unjust for someone else to pay the punishment for the crimes you are guilty of.

As far as I know, you are the only one who has ever said to me that it is entirely unjust for someone else to pay for crimes of which another is guilty. I have to conclude that you made this statement rashly, and without too much thought. There is nothing at all unjust about any father stepping in and paying a speeding fine for his son. It happens all the time, and the judge has no concerns about where the payment comes from, as long as it is lawful money.

How would you react if you were guilty of violating civil law, and your dad loved you so much that he sold his house and spent all of his hard-earned savings to pay the massive fine so that you could get out of prison? Would you point at your father and accuse him of some sort of crime? How perverse would that be? If you did that, you would not only be despising his incredible sacrifice, but you would also reveal something horrible about your own character.

That's what you are doing when you accuse Almighty God of being unjust. He became a man in Jesus of Nazareth to take the punishment for the sin of the world, so that we could live forever. If you or I accuse Him of being unjust, it reveals something horrible about *our* character. We need to humble ourselves, get on our knees, and thank God for giving us life in the first place, and then for offering wicked humanity such an unspeakable gift.

Do you really believe the Holocaust was God's punishment of the Jews?

I would never say that God used Hitler to punish the Jews. If God treated any of us justly and punished us according to our sins, we would all be in Hell in an instant. I'm Jewish and I am as guilty as any Gentile of violating His law.

However, you and I get to stay alive for a time because God is rich in mercy, is filled with what the Bible calls "lovingkindness," and He particularly lavished this loving-kindness upon the Jewish nation. If you study the Scriptures, you will see that He promised them that if they loved and obeyed Him He would give them long life, health, prosperity, and protection from their enemies.

But He also warned that if they disobeyed Him, His hand of protection would be removed. This happened when they were conquered by the Babylonian nation.

When you read Jeremiah and Lamentations, you will see that they were starved, raped, and horribly murdered. The Babylonians were incredibly cruel — they hanged people by one hand, ripped babies from mothers' wombs, committed genocide, and used slave labor. They, like the Nazis, were merciless. The Nazis were trying to eliminate what they believed were "lesser races." Darwin promoted this idea in his book *The Descent of Man*.

Yet with all their sins, God was still rich in mercy and He promised that He would draw the Jewish people back from where He had scattered them throughout the world (see Nehemiah 1:8; Luke 21:24). He said that He would give them their own homeland. That happened in 1948 when they became a nation in one day, as the Scriptures said they would:

> Who has heard such a thing? Who has seen such things? Shall the earth be made to give birth in one day? Or shall a nation be born at once? For as soon as Zion was in labor, she gave birth to her children (Isaiah 66:8).

This accurately describes what happened on May 14, 1948. The Zionist Jews declared independence for an Israeli sovereign nation for the first time in 2,900 years. Hours beforehand a United Nations mandate expired, ending British control of the land. During a 24-hour span of time, foreign control of the land of Israel formally ceased. Israel was literally born in a single day.

Within hours of the declaration of independence in 1948, Israel was attacked by the surrounding countries of Egypt, Jordan, Syria, Lebanon, Iraq, and Saudi Arabia.

Right now the Jews are still surrounded by enemies who are sworn to their death as a nation. Their only hope is to turn to God with their whole heart, and if they obey Him, they will have victory. Only time will tell us if they have learned anything from history.

I want an explanation from God regarding my dad's motor neuron disease, my friend's father raping her, and the chap in Belfast who was hacked to death in front of his wife I read about on Google today. All of which is not my fault and God had the power to stop it. God also has the power to heal my dad, resurrect that murdered guy, though I'm not sure how God would solve the rape thing.

I'm very sorry to hear about your dad and his sickness. It must be heartbreaking. I lost my dad a few years ago.

If you want an explanation from God, you need to read Genesis 3 and Romans 5. We are in a sin-cursed world because Adam sinned and we *all* sin, too. But we are in this mess due to sin, not because God made the world this way. God originally made everything perfect (Genesis 1:31; Dueteronomy 32:4) and it is *our* fault the world is like this. But take heart, this is why Jesus stepped into history — to save us from sin and death. Only Christians have something to look forward to (see Revelation 21 and 22).

But to your important question: You think that God should somehow prevent evil. He should actually stop the murderer and the rapist. This is because you (understandably) consider those two acts to be evil. How about the liar and the thief, the fornicator, pornographer, blasphemer, and the adulterer? Do you think that they are evil and should be stopped? God considers them to be extremely evil. But that's where conversion comes in (the new birth spoken of in John 3). God miraculously removes the hatred from the heart. He changes us on the inside so that we want to stop doing all evil.

So how sincere are you in your desire to see evil stopped? Are you prepared to start with yourself?

Any Christians out there want to take on why the Bible has such a low opinion of women? The Bible is so much more damaging to society in that regard than porn, in my opinion.

You obviously don't know your Bible, or perhaps you have been visiting atheist websites and getting a lopsided view of the Scriptures from a few verses from the Old Testament. The Bible highly esteems women. Take the time to read the Book of Ruth or the Book of Esther and other parts of the Old Testament, where women are portrayed as heroes. Or read Proverbs 31 to see the incredible virtues of a liberated, hardworking, much-loved wife and businesswoman.

Then read in the New Testament about how Jesus treated women with the utmost respect — the "sinful" woman who washed His feet, and the one who was caught in the act of adultery. Or read in the Epistles about how husbands are instructed to love their wives as much as they love their own bodies.

Most women have no idea how men talk about them when they are not around — how they boast of their sexual exploits. So I would suggest that you take the time to read the Bible and see how God's Word honors the fairer sex, while much of a godless world treats women as sex objects to be used and then discarded.

Sorry, Ray, I do not take my morals from a God who drowns opposing armies in the ocean, killed every living thing on earth in a global flood, punished humanity for all time for eating a piece of fruit, rained fire and brimstone on entire cities because he didn't like their behavior, killed the first born of an entire nation, and murdered his own son. Thank God he does not exist.

It seems that you don't know your Bible. God didn't "kill every living thing on earth in a global flood." He allowed sea life, land animals on the ark, and a family of eight people to be saved. He didn't punish humanity "for all time for eating a piece of fruit." Adam was punished for his "disobedience" (see Romans 5:19). If you refuse God's mercy, you too will be punished for your disobedience, not for Adam's.

You are also wrong when you said that "God murdered His own Son." The Bible says that God was in Christ reconciling the world to Himself. Jesus of Nazareth was the Creator in human form (see John 1:1; 1 Timothy 3:16). The reason God became a man was to suffer for the sin of the world (taking the punishment that is due us). We violated God's law (the Ten Commandments), and Jesus paid our fine. That means you can have your case dismissed. It means you can escape Hell, and receive everlasting life as a gift from God (see Romans 6:23).

God warned the pharaoh ten times that He would judge Egypt, and you pinpointed the reason for God drowning his army. It was because it was an "opposing" army. That's a good lesson for us: oppose and you lose. Like Pharaoh, you have been warned (through the Ten Commandments) that God will judge the world because it is at war with Him (see James 4:4). If you refuse to surrender, and you carry on with your rebellion, God will give you over to what the Bible calls a "reprobate mind." I would hate for that to happen to you.

You are right, though, about the fire and brimstone. The same justice of God that fell on Sodom and Gomorrah abides on you (see John 3:36), believe it or not. Please think about your eternal salvation. There's nothing more important.

Ray, what is wrong with using 'filthy language'? Biblically or otherwise? Words are words, and it is you who projects meaning onto them. "Filthiness" is a category that certain words are intentionally used to carry, meaning that if (for example) the entire human race forgot the filthy words of today, new ones would pop up to take their place in the semantic vacuum. But I ask again, what's wrong with using the f-word (filthy word)?

If you are an atheist, you can't say anything is morally "wrong." Is rape wrong? If you answer yes, I ask you, "Who says?" If you say, "Society," then if society deemed rape morally okay, does it become right? What about murder? Is that right or wrong? What *if* society says it's right, just for getting rid of Jews and darker-skinned people? Is it then right? Is it morally okay to kill children in the womb? You say again, "If society says so." How about men marrying men? If society says so. Is pedophilia wrong? Same scenario.

You have no rock to stand on. We do. The rock upon which the Christian stands is immovable, and it will judge all of humanity (including you) on the Day of Judgment (see Romans 2:12). We have the solid rock of the law of God. The commandments were written in stone, and they are unchanging. They tell us that murder is morally wrong, and so are adultery, fornication, lust, greed, envy, and pride. Everything that violates the spirit of God's law is morally wrong (see Romans 7:14). That includes what the Bible calls "filthy language" (see Colossians 3:8).

A recent study found that the use of filthy language tends to help certain people deal with pain:

> The researchers enlisted 64 undergraduate volunteers and had them submerge their hand in a tub of ice water for as long as possible while repeating a swear word of their choice. The experiment was then repeated with the

volunteer repeating a more common word that they would use to describe a table. Contrary to what the researcher expected, the volunteers kept their hands submerged longer while repeating the swear word.[13]

All these researchers found was that certain human beings with a filthy mouth (subconsciously) place value on filthy talk. No doubt blasphemy was included in their language.

> But those things which proceed out of the mouth come from the heart, and they defile a man. For out of the heart proceed evil thoughts, murders, adulteries, fornications, thefts, false witness, blasphemies (Matthew 15:18–19).

Now please explain why there has NEVER been a single substantiated report of a single amputee that regained his amputated limb back from God. Why God does not heal amputees?

How does he know that this has never happened in history, or somewhere else other than in his very limited world? The best he can offer is that he has never heard of such a thing.

His broad statement is typical of those who adamantly say that there is no God. In reality, they don't know that God doesn't exist. So they need to sit at the feet of the learned professor Dawkins and stay with the word "probably."

The question comes with the presupposition that God has never healed even one amputee. The questioner assumes that he has all knowledge of all things that God has done since the creation of the world. He knows what has happened throughout history in Africa, India, China, Russia, and every country on earth, since the beginning of time. He claims "divine omniscience."

It would be more humble for him to say, "With the very limited knowledge that I have of the works of God throughout history, I believe that there has never been a medically substantiated case of Him healing someone whose limb (or any body part) had been amputated. I really don't know if He has or if He hasn't, but I still come to the conclusion that He doesn't exist."

I have to admit, though, that if God *did* heal an amputee today, it would be nothing short of a miracle. If He created a moving, living human arm, filled with incredibly complex and responding muscles, joined to an unbelievably complex hand, with a mass of blood vessels filled with life-giving blood, that connects to a pumping human heart, with an amazingly intricate nervous system that responds to the phenomenal human brain, it would be an "evident" miracle. It would be absolute and undeniable proof that He does indeed exist. Conceded.

Take a moment to look downward and slightly to your right. There (unless you are an amputee) you should see a living human arm. Bend it at the middle. Now slowly pull it up toward your eyes. Focus and look at it. Think for a few moments about the amazing ability of Almighty God. Listen carefully to the God-given voice of "reason." You are not an animal. You have the ability to reason. No animal can do this in a way that a human being can. Then, while still listening to that voice, slowly read this Bible verse: "And one of them struck the servant of the high priest and cut off [amputated] his right ear. But Jesus answered and said, 'Permit even this.' And He touched his ear and healed him" (Luke 22:50–51). If, for some reason, you are not hearing the voice of reason, may He do the same to you.

> *Sometimes Ray makes me angry, or annoyed, flabbergasted or concerned for his mental health. But all in all, he is a good man. I wouldn't torture him, make him feel like a horrible useless little sinful piece of garbage, or arbitrarily destroy him on a meteorological whim. I wouldn't call him names or accuse him of greed. My gut feeling is that Ray's not all that bad. Probably.*

I'm glad you used the word "probably." It shows that you think that you could be wrong about me being a good man. And you are. Big time. I'm not a good man, and I am "all that bad." A "good" man loves the God who gave him life — with all of his heart, mind, soul, and strength. He also loves every other human being as much as he loves himself. A good man never lusts after women or has a selfish or unclean thought. He is perfect in thought, word, and in deed.

By human definition of the word "good," I may be good. But man's definition is very low. God's is very high, and it's by His perfect standard of goodness that we will be judged on Judgment Day. Definitely. Consider Christ's statement in Mark 10:18.

No doubt this will make you angry, annoyed, flabbergasted, and very concerned about my mental health. This is because you don't understand God's terrible justice; neither do you understand His amazing mercy. You and I may be a "sinful piece of garbage," but it is on that garbage that God set His love and suffered and died to cleanse us of our filth.

> *When asked, "Do you believe a woman has the right to kill her child in the womb?" one atheist answered: "Nope. A child has the right to live. A blastocyte, however, has the sentient equivalent of a colony of bacteria and it is more morally wrong to slaughter a cow at a slaughterhouse than to kill a blastocyte."*

The Bible is consistent when it refers to a pregnant woman as being "with child." It doesn't say "with fetus" nor does it redefine a child in the womb as a "blastocyte."

We are also told in Scripture that the life of the flesh is in the blood (see Leviticus 17:11). If you lose your blood, you lose your life. The blood is sparked at conception. Therefore life begins at that moment. Take that life and you murder a human being, and no amount of redefinition will change that fact. And if you have murdered another human being, you will stand before God on Judgment Day with the blood of the innocent on your hands (see Proverbs 6:16–17).

A society may redefine its beliefs, but new definitions don't change reality. Hitler redefined the Jews as being less than human, and thus began the efficiency of Nazi Germany. Jewish men, women, and children were marched or sent by train, truck, or bus to a nearby forest. A ditch was dug to serve as a mass grave. The Jews were ordered to remove their clothing, place it in neat piles, and wait. Small groups were then taken down into the pit. One German witness later recalled:

> The pit was already two-thirds full. I estimated that it held a thousand people. I looked for the man who did the shooting. He was an SS man who sat at the edge of the narrow end of the pit, his feet dangling into it. He had a tommy gun on his knees and was smoking a cigarette. The people — they were completely naked — went down some steps . . . to the place where the SS man directed them. They lay down in front of the dead and wounded. Some caressed the living and spoke to them in a low voice. Then I heard a series of shots.[14]

Many Nazis escaped the justice of man, but none will escape the justice of God.

So the next time you advocate the murder of an innocent human being because of your redefinition of life, feel free to wash your hands (as Pontius Pilate did) in water. It won't change a thing.

> Out, damn'd spot! out, I say! — One; two: why, then 'tis time to do't. — Hell is murky. — Fie, my lord, fie, a soldier, and afeard? What need we fear who knows it, when none can call our pow'r to accompt? — Yet who would have thought the old man to have had so much blood in him?[15]

Just where in the Bible does God say that it's wrong to "show half-naked people lying on top of each other in sexually explicit positions?" Didn't God make us born naked? Didn't God make sex? Comfort sounds like a loyal member of the Taliban.

The above reaction was typical of many when I spoke of once covering up pornography on a billboard in my neighborhood with a large orange blanket. I was accused of wanting to cover up women with "burkas."

On the contrary, there's nothing at all wrong with looking at attractive women. God made the female form to be attractive to men. However, He did say that looking at a woman with lust is to commit adultery in the heart (see Matthew 5:27–28). Looking and lusting are two different things.

Covering a woman with a veil doesn't deal with lust because it's an issue of the human imagination, and the sinful imagination of man isn't stopped by a mere veil. It is the heart of man that is evil, not the naked body of a woman. Lust made its entry when Adam and Eve sinned in the Garden of Eden. Until that time they were naked, and they had the approving smile of God. When He commanded them to "multiply," He wasn't talking about math.

I have a question for those of you who would gladly put a national ban on any form of censorship. If a clothing manufacturer embarked on a billboard campaign showing naked adults in sexually explicit positions with underage individuals, would you object, or would you be an advocate for their freedom of sexual expression?

If you are an advocate of child pornography, I would appreciate you giving me your name and address. I think there are people in your neighborhood who should be warned that you live in their area.

I would hope that you would strongly object to a billboard campaign that uses child porn. If that's the case, then you do believe in some form of censorship, and you do have a moral divide. You believe that certain things are morally wrong. It's just that your moral divide is very low. God's is very high.

I was also encouraged to move to places like Amsterdam, where there is sexual freedom, hardly any crime, and where atheists are rampant. However, back in 2008 *Newsweek* reported:

> Amsterdam plans to close down its most famous district, citing sleaze, criminal activity, and human trafficking. . . . [Because] too many brothels and sex bars are linked to criminality, the authorities plan to all but erase the Red Light District.[16]

The clean-up plan was approved by an overwhelming 43 to 2 majority.

Still, it takes more than censorship of a Red Light District to deal with lust in the hearts of sinful men. It takes the power of God through the message of the gospel. He can forgive each one of us and change us so that we want to do that which is pleasing in His sight.

All it takes to be forgiven and cleansed is a little honesty. One atheist reminded me of that fact when he said, "I have never lusted over a woman . . . I have never lusted," and then added, "I'll make no bones about my use of pornography."

When God kills someone, that's holy and good. And when he orders someone killed, that's also holy and good. And when he alters hearts so that he can use someone as an example, that's holy and good, too. Because God is holy and good he can be as evil as he likes because it's holy and good.

It is amazing to me that an atheist will use the word "evil" when it suits him, even if it's just in sarcasm. In reality he has no definition of the word. Evil cannot exist in their worldview; otherwise their worldview is wrong. Neither can good. Those who would argue with such a thought will be quick to claim that it is *society* (not God) that defines good and evil.

But if society dictates that it is good to kill children in the womb, over the time of one generation the "morality" of the society moves abortion from being something that is considered evil to something that is good and right. If the government (society) says homosexuals marrying each other is good, it moves from one generation believing it is evil to the next believing it is good and acceptable.

If the government says it's okay to kill Spaniards, Swedes, Jews, and homosexuals because only the fit should survive, what is morally evil changes to that which is morally good in their eyes.

Those who know their Bibles will know that this was the historical track record of Israel. Once a generation forsook God's law (the definition of good and evil) they predictably became lawless because they had no absolute meaning for what was good and evil (see Isaiah 5:20–21 and Judges 17:6).

But there is a paradox when an atheist makes a moral judgment about the character of God. He does so out of a blind self-righteousness. He is burning with unlawful sexual desire (lust), is a liar, and thief, a blasphemer, filled with ingratitude for the God-given gift of life, and yet he has the audacity to point a holier-than-thou finger at Almighty God and accuse Him of sin. Such is the epitome of hypocrisy.

Let's see who the guilty party is on Judgment Day.

Thomas Edison is one of my all-time heroes. I love his enthusiasm, tenacity, insight, and wit. You will frequently find his famous name along with his famous words, along with Galileo, Abraham Lincoln, Albert Einstein, and others, on atheist websites. None of these men were atheists, but they are listed on atheist sites. This is because it's hard to find anyone famous and respected who didn't believe that God existed.

It was Edison who said, "I do not believe in the God of the theologians; but that there is a Supreme Intelligence I do not doubt."[17] He didn't doubt for a moment that there was an intelligent Creator. Design is absolute proof of a Designer.

In August of 1931, as Edison was slipping into death, he was asked if he had thought about a life hereafter. He replied, "It does not matter. No one knows."[18] This is a very common response, and it reveals that the person, intelligent though he may be, isn't thinking too deeply.

Those who make the statement, "No one knows," are revealing that they think they know what everyone knows. There are more than six billion people on the earth, and they know what everyone knows and what they don't know. Sure.

Edison also said, "We don't know a millionth of one percent about anything."[19] His darkness when it came to the issue of eternity was self-imposed. It certainly does matter. Light is there for those who seek it. Jesus said, "I am the light of the world. He who follows Me shall not walk in darkness, but have the light of life" (John 8:12). It's a tragedy that his tenacity didn't extend to what really matters. We can live without the light bulb but not without the Light of the World — Jesus Christ.

For some time now, believers in evolution have been goading me to define biological evolution and comment on "the scientific method." I haven't, for a good reason. *Talk Origins* says this about the definition of "evolution":

> Unfortunately the common definitions of evolution outside of the scientific community are different. For example, in the *Oxford Concise Science Dictionary* we find the following definition:

> > Evolution: The gradual process by which the present diversity of plant and animal life arose from the earliest and most primitive organisms, which is believed to have been continuing for the past 3,000 million years.

> This is inexcusable for a dictionary of science. Not only does this definition exclude prokaryotes, protozoa, and fungi, but it specifically includes the term "gradual process," which should not be part of the definition. More importantly, the definition seems to refer more to the history of evolution than to evolution itself. Using this definition, it is possible to debate whether evolution is still occurring, but the definition provides no easy way of distinguishing evolution from other processes. For example, is the increase in height among Caucasians over the past several hundred years an example of evolution? Are the

color changes in the peppered moth population examples of evolution? This is not a scientific definition.

Standard dictionaries are even worse:

> "Evolution: . . . the doctrine according to which higher forms of life have gradually arisen out of lower." — Chambers

> "Evolution: . . . the development of a species, organism, or organ from its original or primitive state to its present or specialized state; phylogeny or ontogeny." — Webster's[20]

I haven't defined what I believe is biological evolution because I don't believe it took place. Neither have I defined it according to what believers believe it is, because they can't agree on a standard definition. The science dictionary doesn't have it right. Neither do the standard dictionaries.

So who has the correct definition? The answer is that *you* do. Evolution is anything you want it to be. It's bacteria evolving. It's mutations evolving into ordered life. It's variations *within* species. It's changes in fruit flies or moths. It's differing traits passed down from your parents. It's the belief that all creation has a common ancestor, when any similarities in creation don't prove common descent, they prove a common Creator.

The advantage of multiple and confusing definitions is that you can change what it is, any time you wish, to anything you want. When biologists discover that the fossil record shows an abrupt appearance (as the Bible teaches), they simply redefine evolution to include "punctuated equilibrium." There are no rules. No confines.

The scientific method must be observable. Evolution isn't. Anything that is observed is based on the presupposition that evolution took place. If a believer believes it happened, he will see evolution everywhere.

But even the legitimately observable can't be conclusive. If scientists observed and counted ten million white swans, can they say conclusively that all swans are white? Of course not. One black swan destroys the theory.

Darwinian evolution doesn't even have one white swan. All it has is an idea — a failed one.

P.S. The writer on *Talk Origins* gives *what he believes* is the accurate definition of evolution. It's the accurate one because *he* says so. Again, the science dictionary is wrong. Standard dictionaries are wrong. He is right.

GENESIS 2:1

2 Thus the heavens and the earth, and all the host of them, were finished.

2 ᵇ And on the seventh day God ended His work which He had done, and He rested on the seventh day from all His work which He had done. ³ Then God b the seventh day and

Chapter Two

The Bible: Biblical and Theological Issues

I just wanted to reiterate that it's important to remember that all six million of Hitler's Jewish victims are definitely in hell, according to Christian theology.

To say that all six million Jews who died in the Holocaust are in Hell is a twisted interpretation of Christian theology. I am a Jew, and I became a Christian. Jesus was Jewish. The disciples were Jewish. The first 8,000 converts were Jewish. Christianity went "to the Jew first." It came *through* the Jews, from the land of the Jews, to the Jews. Any Jew who believes the Scriptures will come to Christ. Those who don't, won't.

Why then would anyone say that all Jews who died at the hands of Nazis are in Hell? Presumably it's because they are offended that Jesus spoke of the exclusive nature of salvation. He said, "I am the way, the truth and the life. No one comes to the Father except through Me" (John 14:6). That is exclusive, but that is what the Jewish disciples preached to their Jewish hearers: "Nor is there salvation in any other, for there is no other name under heaven given among men by which we must be saved" (Acts 4:12). This is the teaching of the Jew who (under the inspiration of the God of the Jews) wrote, "Whoever transgresses and does not abide in the doctrine of Christ does not have God. He who abides in the doctrine of Christ has both the Father and the Son" (2 John 1:9). When God spoke to the Jews in their Scriptures, He promised to give them "one way":

> Behold, I will gather them out of all countries where I have driven them in My anger, in My fury, and in great wrath; I will bring them back to this place, and I will cause them to dwell safely. They shall be My people, and I will be their God: then I will give them one heart and one way, that they may fear Me forever, for the good of them and their children after them. And I will make an everlasting covenant with them, that I will not turn away from doing them good; but I will put My fear in their hearts so that they will not depart from Me (Jeremiah 32:37–40).

So if you are offended that there is only one way to God, your argument is with Him.

The moral law (which was given to the Jews) leaves each of us guilty before God, and any attempt on our part to offer Him good works through religious works (praying, fasting, doing good, etc.) is not "good works" at all but attempts to bribe the Judge. Scripture teaches that those who offer religious works are motivated by a guilty conscience (see Hebrews 10:22), and we are also warned that God will not be bribed (see Proverbs 15:8). The only way for us to be saved from Hell (our just punishment under God's law) is if the Judge extends mercy. That's what happened at the Cross. God in Christ was paying our fine so that our case could legally be dismissed. When anyone repents and trusts the God-given Savior, he or she receives forgiveness of sins and the gift of everlasting life (see Romans 6:23). Salvation from death is exclusive to Christ, but open to all (see Acts 2:21). It is open to the Jew and the Gentile, to those who are black or white, to the wise and to the fool. Many atheists have become Christians, but before they could do so they had to make one small change (see Hebrews 11:6). It is easier for a needle to go through the eye of a camel than for an atheist to enter the kingdom of God. Psalm 10:4 tells us why: "The wicked in his proud countenance does not seek God; God is in none of his thoughts."

A recent discovery showed that self-replicating RNA strands could come from elements found during the conditions of early earth. Besides — isn't it the belief of creationists such as yourself that God created man (life) out of dust (non-life)? Doesn't this also mean that life was created from non-life?

Man had no life until God breathed it into him. He was nothing but a corpse until the life of God entered his inanimate body: "And the LORD God formed man of the dust of the ground, and breathed into his nostrils the breath of life; and man became a living being" (Genesis 2:7). All living things have their source in God, who is the eternal fountain of life.

The Gospel of John says that Jesus Christ (called "the Word") was "in the beginning with God" when life on earth began, and that "all things were made through Him" (see John 1:1–4). Then it says that the "Word became flesh and dwelt among us" (John 1:14). If you look at the opening verses of Genesis 1 you will repeatedly see, "Then God said . . ." (Genesis 1:3). It was the spoken word that brought creation into being.

Then this "Word" that created all thing became flesh, and the Bible says, "In Him was life" (John 1:4). This is why Jesus said strange things about His words. He said, "The words that I speak to you are spirit, and *they are life* (see John 6:63; italics added). He claimed to be the very source of life itself:

> "I am the way, the truth, and the life" (John 14:6).
> "I am the resurrection and the life" (John 11:25).
> "I have come that they may have life" (John 10:10).
> "I am the bread of Life" (John 6:35).

> The Apostle Paul said, "Christ who is our life . . ." (see Colossians 3:4).

Look at what the Bible says of who (or what) Jesus was:

> That which was from the beginning, which we have heard, which we have seen with our eyes, which we have looked upon, and our hands have handled, concerning the Word of life — the life was manifested, and we have seen, and bear witness, and declare to you that eternal life which was with the Father and was manifested to us (1 John 1:1–2).

> For as the Father has life in Himself, so He has granted the Son to have life in Himself (John 5:26).

So when people "receive Christ," they aren't receiving some dead religion or some sort of an intellectual belief. They are actually receiving the very source of life itself. That's why Scripture says, "He who has the Son has life" (1 John 5:12). Do you have the life of Christ within you (see Colossians 1:27), or are you still "dead in trespasses and sins" (Ephesians 2:1)?

Nowhere in the Old Testament is there any hint of eternal punishment after death. There are occasional hints of an afterlife for the righteous, but none of an afterlife, in Hell or elsewhere, for the wicked. The New Testament, of course, has many mentions of post-death punishment, another change in the account of how God treats His creatures.

Skeptics have argued that any Old Testament reference to the word "hell" simply refers to the grave, or to a burning trash heap outside of Jerusalem. This is the scholarly way they put it: "Hell is always translated from the Hebrew word *Sheol* (which is used 65 times in the Old Testament) and means simply 'the world of the dead.' There is no hint of a place of fire. *Sheol* is translated as 'grave' 31 times, 'hell' 31 times, and 'pit' 3 times."

Upon the wicked he will rain coals; fire and brimstone and a burning wind shall be the portion of their cup (Psalm 11:6).

You shall make them as a fiery oven in the time of Your anger: the LORD shall swallow them up in his wrath, and the fire shall devour them (Psalm 21:9).

Let burning coals fall upon them; let them be cast into the fire, into deep pits, that they rise not up again (Psalm 140:10).

For a fire is kindled in My anger, and shall burn to the lowest hell; it shall consume the earth with her increase, and set on fire the foundations of the mountains (Deuteronomy 32:22).

The wicked shall be turned into hell, and all the nations that forget God (Psalm 9:17).

Let death seize them, let them go down alive into hell, for wickedness is in their dwellings and among them (Psalm 55:15).

If I ascend into heaven, You are there; if I make my bed in hell, behold, You are there (Psalm 139:8).

Her feet go down to death, her steps lay hold of hell (Proverbs 5:5).

Her house is the way to hell, descending to the chambers of death (Proverbs 7:27).

But he does not know that the dead are there, that her guests are in the depths of hell (Proverbs 9:18).

Hell and destruction are before the LORD; so how much more the hearts of the sons of men? (Proverbs 15:11)

The way of life winds upward for the wise, that he may turn away from hell below (Proverbs 15:24).

You shall beat him with a rod, and deliver his soul from hell (Proverbs 23:14).

Hell and destruction are never full; so the eyes of man are never satisfied (Proverbs 27:20).

And many of those who sleep in the dust of the earth shall awake, some to everlasting life, some to shame and everlasting contempt (Daniel 12:2).

Hell from beneath is excited about you, to meet you at your coming; it stirs up the dead for you, all the chief ones of the earth; it has raised up from their thrones all the kings of the nations (Isaiah 14:9).

Yet you shall be brought down to Sheol, to the lowest depths of the Pit (Isaiah 14:15).

I made the nations shake at the sound of its fall, when I cast it down to hell together with those who descend into the Pit; and all the trees of Eden, the choice and best of Lebanon, all that drink water, were comforted in the depths of the earth. They also went down to hell with it, with those slain by the sword; and those who were its strong arm dwelt in its shadows among the nations (Ezekiel 31:16–17).

The strong among the mighty shall speak to him out of the midst of hell with those who help him: they are gone down, they lie with the uncircumcised, slain by the sword (Ezekiel 32:21).

Though they dig into hell, from there My hand shall take them; though they climb up to heaven, from there I will bring them down (Amos 9:2).

Indeed, because he transgresses by wine, he is a proud man, and he does not stay at home. Because he enlarges his desire as hell, and he is like death, and cannot be satisfied, he gathers to himself all nations and heaps up for himself all peoples (Habakkuk 2:5).

The New Testament made a reference to those who dilute the Word of God: "Which untaught and unstable people twist to their own destruction, as they do also the rest of the Scriptures" (2 Peter 3:16). So you have some choices to make. You can say that God doesn't exist, which (in the light of creation) is unspeakably foolish. You can say that God exists but that He doesn't care about justice, which is idolatry (that would mean that Hitler's punishment for the slaughter of six million Jews was to simply die and know nothing). Then again, you can believe the soothing words of those who twist Scripture and say that Hell doesn't exist. Or you can take warning from the Bible that God will see that ultimate justice is ultimately done, repent, and trust the Savior, who warned in the New Testament:

If your hand or foot causes you to sin, cut it off and cast it from you. It is better for you to enter into life lame or maimed, rather than having two hands or two feet, to be cast into the everlasting fire. And if your eye causes you to sin, pluck it out and cast it from you. It is better for you to enter into life with one eye, rather than having two eyes, to be cast into hell fire (Matthew 18:8–9).[21]

If the Bible is always right and never needs updating, why is there a New Testament? Why don't boys have to be circumcised now? Why can you eat pork? Why can you work on a Saturday? Why don't you have to batter people's skulls in with stones who worship "false gods"?

One of the most common mistakes people make with the Bible is to confuse the issues of Law and grace. The Scriptures make the difference when they say, "The Law was given through Moses, but grace and truth came through Jesus Christ" (John 1:17). The Law of Moses is categorized into three parts: the moral law (the Ten Commandments), the civil law (the law for Israel's court system), and the ceremonial law (the law for ceremonial worship). The whole Law had 613 precepts (its do's and don'ts).

Male circumcision was part of the ceremonial law given to Israel to set them apart from other nations, as was not eating pork and Sabbath worship. Capital punishment under the Law — for murder, adultery, idolatry, and blasphemy — was part of the civil law of Israel, so why should we as a nation live under the standards of justice given to a nation three thousand years ago? Through grace, we are under no obligation to keep any of the dietary, civil, or ceremonial laws of Israel. The moral Law is transcendental; that is, it was always in effect. For example, Cain killed Abel — it was murder and it was wrong, prior to Moses presenting the Law.

However, we are under obligation to keep the moral Law. It was given to Israel but its purpose is that "all the world may become guilty before God" (see Romans 3:19–20). And it certainly does.

When we study its holy precepts and understand that we violate the seventh by our lust, it shows us we need the grace (mercy) of God.

The reason the moral Law leaves us guilty before God is that its precepts are written on our hearts, via the conscience. We intuitively know that it is wrong to lie, steal, lust, murder, commit adultery, etc. The Law reveals sin, and Christ covers sin (the New Testament fulfills the Old Testament).

It was one night way back in 1972 that the Law showed me that I was guilty and heading for Hell, and it sent me to the Savior where I found mercy. The Law came by Moses, but grace and truth came by Jesus Christ. As the hymnwriters wrote many years ago:

> By God's grace at last my sin I learned,
> Then I trembled at the Law I spurned,
> Till my guilty soul imploring turned, to Calvary.[22]

So, Ray, I have a question for you. How did the 16,000 or so kinds on Noah's ark become the 1.4 million species today?

"Species" is a man-made term for classifications. Species is basically variation within the kinds. For example, there is one dog kind but we classify them as several species, such as wolves, coyotes, dingoes, domestic dogs, etc., but they can all interbreed. So there is still the same basic number of kinds (some have gone extinct).

Now if you do like to ask difficult questions, ask an atheist how the 1.4 million species came from nothing. Despite his protests, that's what he believes. When he says that he doesn't know how everything began, ask him how is it that each of the 1.4 million species evolved both male and female — how they reproduced before that time, and why females evolved anyway, if things were buzzing along with just males. Press him on the issue. Make him think about what he believes. Then ask him if he can make a bird from nothing. When he says that nobody can, call him on his intellectual dishonesty in his belief that nothing made everything. Believing all the strange things in the Bible is a breeze compared to the fantasies the average atheist believes.

Hey, Ray. Lust, greed, lies, blasphemy, theft. All of these things can be found in the Bible and then some. Gotta love that old time religion!

The Bible has a whole lot more than lust, greed, lies, blasphemy, and theft in its many pages. It's full of adultery, murder, rape, jealousy, pride, incest, homosexuality, fornication, and torture, just to name a few.

Perhaps you are not aware that the Scriptures mainly relate the history of the Hebrew nation. It begins with the creation of the first male and female and their tragic fall from fellowship with their Creator. This didn't come because of the eating of an apple. It came through the sin of disobedience. Then Scripture traces the same rebellion as it manifested itself in the whole human race. The Bible doesn't hide the sinful heart of man. It exposes each man's wickedness and warns that God has appointed a day in which He will judge the world in righteousness. So whatever you do, don't make the mistake of writing off the Bible as being evil, when it simply exposes evil. Has it exposed the evil in your heart yet, or aren't you aware of it?

The amazing thing about this collection of 66 books is that their common thread (through the Old Testament) is God's promise to release mankind from his greatest enemy — death itself. The New Testament tells us how He did it. See John 3:17–18 for details.

The God of the Old Testament ordered genocide. He was, as Richard Dawkins so rightly stated, "a vindictive, bloodthirsty ethnic cleanser; a misogynistic, homophobic, racist, infanticidal, genocidal, filicidal, pestilential, megalomaniacal, sadomasochistic, capriciously malevolent bully."[23]

As justification for God's merciless judgment against the Canaanites, we are told by Bible scholars that they were a morally corrupt people. They sacrificed children, had sex with animals and their parents, etc. To see a full list of sins, read Leviticus 18. The religion of the Canaanites was a fertility cult. They turned their women into temple prostitutes, and they sacrificed their children by fire in the white-hot arms of their pagan gods.

To get this into perspective we have to look at our own nation in regard to homosexuality, adultery, fornication, pornography, and violence. We have murdered more than *50 million* innocent babies in the womb! How bad does a nation have to get for God Himself to order the slaughter of every man, woman, and child? Why didn't God intervene when Hitler's evil regime was in power and kill off the German nation before it slaughtered millions of innocent people across the world? He *did* intervene with the Canaanites once their sin reached its full measure (Genesis 15:16). The same could be said of the Nazis. Once their sin reached a certain point, Allied forces were able to remove them from power. So how can we begin to understand this specific and harsh judgment?

The first key is to realize that the God of the New Testament is the same as He was in the Old Testament. He never changes (see Malachi 3:6). In the New Testament we are told to fear Him because He has the power to kill the body and cast the soul into Hell (see Luke 12:5), and the New Testament has enough judgments in it to make us fear Him. Take for one example His fearful judgments against wicked humanity in the Book of Revelation.

The reason we should fear God is because He *is* to be feared. He is still the same today as He was in the New Testament, and He will be the same on Judgment Day. He's not going to compromise eternal justice just because sinful man points a holier-than-thou finger at Him in moral judgment. We have more chance of changing the inner core temperature of the sun because we don't like the fact that it's hot. However, those who insist on standing in moral judgment over God do so because they are making two serious mistakes: (1) they haven't seen God as He is, and (2) they haven't seen themselves as they are.

This is what God Himself said to wicked humanity when they continued to do evil: "These things you have done and I kept silent; you thought I was once entirely like you" (Psalm 50:21; AMP).

Humanity's mistake is that we think that God is something like us. We *are* made in the "image" of God, in that we are moral beings, but God is much more. And we are in a fallen sate of sin.

One way to illustrate the difference is to consider the subject of crime. If a man threatens to beat his dog, there's no real consequence for his threat. If he threatens to beat up a police officer, he will more than likely appear before a judge for threatening an officer of the law. However, if he threatens the president of the United States, he will find himself in prison for a long time. It is the *same* crime, but the *penalty* increases because of the importance of the one against whom the crime is committed.

When any of us commit a sin, we commit a crime against Almighty God. Jesus spoke about where sin originates when He said, "For out of the heart proceed evil thoughts, murders, adulteries, fornications, thefts, false witness, blasphemies" (Matthew 15:19). Ask human beings if they think those sins are serious, and most will say that there's not much wrong with evil thoughts, fornication, blasphemy, and lying. They will say things like, "Who hasn't told white lies, or taken something small that belongs to someone else? *Everybody* does it." Those sins aren't seen as being too serious because they are seen from the low moral standards of humanity.

But God is absolute and perfect holiness, and He sees each of those crimes as being so serious that they demand the death penalty and damnation in Hell. Without the help of the Holy Spirit to give us understanding, we will always see these sins as trivial, but on the Day of Judgment when we stand in the presence of a Holy Creator, we will see how terribly serious they are.

Jesus spoke of sin as being so deadly that if our eye causes us to so much as lust, we should pluck it out and cast it from us. Obviously He was speaking metaphorically to show us how gravely serious sin is in the sight of God. With that in mind, carefully read what Scripture says about this issue:

> If your hand causes you to sin, cut it off. It is better for you to enter into life maimed, rather than having two hands, to go to hell, into the fire that shall never be quenched — where
>
> "Their worm does not die
>
> And the fire is not quenched."
>
> And if your foot causes you to sin, cut it off. It is better for you to enter life lame, rather than having two feet, to be cast into hell, into the fire that shall never be quenched — where
>
> "Their worm does not die
>
> And the fire is not quenched."
>
> And if your eye causes you to sin, pluck it out. It is better for you to enter the kingdom of God with one eye, rather than having two eyes, to be cast into hell fire — where
>
> "Their worm does not die
>
> And the fire is not quenched" (Mark 9:43–48).

So if God applied His high moral standard to humanity right now, His perfect law would seize upon every one of us, instantly take us to Hell, and absolute and perfect justice would be done.

If Hitler had commanded Joshua to kill every Canaanite, he would have been guilty of the crime of genocide, because Hitler (like you and me) was a sinful man. But God is morally faultless and therefore all of His judgments are righteous and true altogether. I have no idea why God didn't choose to show mercy toward the Canaanites. Perhaps they may have been a nation of potential "Hitlers" and God killed them off before they were able to become a great power. But who am I to question the moral character of Almighty God? I would never be so foolish and presumptuous. But if we do want to understand why God does things, we need to meditate on Romans 11:33: "Oh, the depth of the riches both of the wisdom and knowledge of God! How unsearchable are His judgments and His ways past finding out!"

One more thought. Skeptics often ask, "If God were to tell you to murder people, would you do it?" The answer is that I definitely wouldn't. This is because God doesn't tell His children to murder people. This is how I know:

> God, who at various times and in various ways spoke in time past to the fathers by the prophets, has in these last days spoken to us by His Son, whom He has appointed heir of all things, through whom also He made the worlds (Hebrews 1:1–2).

I speak to God through prayer, and He speaks to me specifically through His Son. Here then is how I should treat other people:

But I say to you who hear: Love your enemies, do good to those who hate you, bless those who curse you, and pray for those who spitefully use you. To him who strikes you on the one cheek, offer the other also. And from him who takes away your cloak, do not withhold your tunic either. Give to everyone who asks of you. And from him who takes away your goods do not ask them back (Luke 6:27–30).

Why would anyone question the killing of innocent men, women, and children? The obvious answer is that it is morally wrong. But the atheist can't say that *anything* is morally wrong, because he doesn't believe in moral absolutes. His predictable answer is that it is society that dictates right from wrong. So if a society deemed it legal to exterminate Jews, then it becomes morally okay? It must, if it is mob rule that dictates ethics. The answer is that our knowledge of what is right and wrong must trace itself back to God and to His moral law. *The reason we are horrified at the thought of genocide is because we are made in His image.* My dog couldn't care less about genocide. Neither could my chickens. In fact, *none* of the animal kingdom has the inbuilt knowledge of morality to a point where they set up court systems and administer justice to their fellow creatures. Only man does that.

So make sure that you're not so foolish as to reject God's gift of eternal life just because you think that He is morally corrupt and that you are righteous. On Judgment Day you will discover that God is just and that you, like the rest of us, are desperately wicked.

According to the Christian model, Hitler, as far as anyone knows, could very well be in Heaven right now, enjoying the fruits of his last-minute redemption.

There's a game that's often played by skeptics. They create hypothetical scenarios so that they can (in their own minds) justify rejection of the gospel.

A drug addict is dying because of a disease that is related to his addiction. But when a faithful doctor takes the time to point out the evident symptoms that are all over the addict's flesh, he responds by saying that the hideous spots are normal, and that all his friends have them.

The doctor pleads with him to listen and says that a large drug company has developed a cure for the fatal disease. To which the addict says, "What if an elephant fell from the sky and swallowed it before I could get to it? Huh, doc? Huh? What about that? You and your stupid pill! I don't believe the drug company even exists. You idiot. Rather than talk about this so-called disease and your brainless drug company, I want to talk about the age of this medical building."

Why would he act in such a way? The answer is obvious. He loves his addiction. That's why he has disdain for the faithful doctor and the drug company he represents.

> And this is the condemnation, that the light has come into the world, and men loved darkness rather than light, because their deeds were evil. For everyone practicing evil hates the light and does not come to the light, lest his deeds should be exposed (John 3:19–20).

Can you explain to me how these two ideas can peacefully co-exist? 1. God's moral standards are not the same as man's standards. 2. Man's moral standards were defined and then given to us by God. I've pointed this out before but never received a response. I'd very much like to hear an explanation.

The answer is simple. There is only one "moral standard," and that morality is defined by God, not man (e.g., the Ten Commandments). Anything that falls short of their absolute moral perfection is called "sin" (see 1 John 3:4), and all sin will receive just retribution. To put it in secular terms, all who break God's Law will be punished by the Law (see Romans 2:12).

Here now is a testimony to the stupidity of us as human beings. We think that if we don't believe in something, it therefore doesn't exist. Unbelievers say that they don't believe in gods. That is supposed to encompass the God who created them. God doesn't exist because *they* don't believe in Him. Hell doesn't exist because *they* don't believe in it.

If you are an atheist, try an experiment. Go outside at midday on a clear day, look at the sun, and say, "I see no evidence that suns exist." You will notice that the sun doesn't go away. An old Chinese proverb says, "He who gazes upon the sun need not debate its brilliance." The sun exists despite whatever you do or don't believe about it. It's intellectually embarrassing to have to explain this, but unbelief or belief doesn't negate reality.

Creation is the brilliant light that reveals the Creator. His moral standard is revealed in His law, the Ten Commandments, and those commandments are affirmed by your God-given conscience. So there it is — you have before you the offer of life in Jesus Christ through trust in Him, or death and Hell through unbelief (which is rooted in disobedience). See www.needGod.com for details.

It would be of great benefit to skeptics and seekers alike if you would explain why one must not be skeptical when reading the Bible, yet should be skeptical when it comes to evolution. Take as much time as you need, but please answer this question that has been repeatedly asked.

There is a real difference between honest skepticism and what the Bible calls "unbelief." One can be a sincere seeker of truth and the other has what is called "presuppositions." If I open the Bible supposing that it is filled with lies and errors and read it with a hardened heart, then I cut myself off from its light, because you have God's promise that He "resists the proud, but gives grace to the humble" (1 Peter 5:5). If you have a proud heart, God Himself will be in opposition to you.

Look at what happened to two people who were skeptical and asked questions of God. The first is a priest named Zacharias:

> And Zacharias said to the angel, "How shall I know this? For I am an old man, and my wife is well advanced in years." And the angel answered and said to him, "I am Gabriel, who stands in the presence of God, and was sent to speak to you and bring you these glad tidings. But behold, you will be mute and not able to speak until the day these things take place, because you did not believe my words which will be fulfilled in their own time" (Luke 1:18–20).

In this passage of the Bible we see what's behind atheism. It is what the Bible calls the sin of "unbelief." An atheist is someone who has no belief in God or in any gods. So what's wrong with that? Can they help it if they doubt?

Imagine that a father tells his beloved son that he is going to buy him a bike for Christmas. The father carefully explains that it will be a red bike, with gears and high-tech wheels, and that it will be extremely lightweight. He explains to the boy that it's completely paid for and that he will get it as a gift first thing on Christmas morning. What would you think if the son says, "How do I know this will happen?" Such a question would be an insult to his father's integrity. It means that he doesn't trust his own father.

Even the most sinful of us is offended when a person doesn't believe something we tell him or her. When we don't believe people it means that we think they are liars, that they are devious, and that they are therefore not worth trusting.

However, this insult is greatly magnified if we don't believe something *God* says. He is without sin. He is absolutely trustworthy, and He is even incapable of lying (the Bible says that it is "impossible" for God to lie — Hebrews 6:18). This is why "unbelief" is a great sin. It grossly insults the integrity of a holy God, and this is why Gabriel is greatly offended.

When Zacharias insulted him with his unbelief, he stated that he was Gabriel "who stands in the presence of God." This was a five-star general among the angelic hosts. Sinners cannot stand in the presence of God, but this perfectly sinless angel did, and so he struck Zacharias dumb for being so dumb.

Never insult God with your unbelief. The Scriptures say, "He who does not believe God has made Him a liar" (1 John 5:10), and "See to it, brothers, that none of you has a sinful, unbelieving heart that turns away from the living God" (Hebrews 3:12; NIV). Those who don't believe are like Zacharias, after the angel struck him.

Now look at another skeptic named Mary:

> Then Mary said to the angel, "How can this be, since I do not know a man?" And the angel answered and said to her, "The Holy Spirit will come upon you, and the power of the Highest will overshadow you; therefore, also, that Holy One who is to be born will be called the Son of God. Now indeed, Elizabeth your relative has also

conceived a son in her old age; and this is now the sixth month for her who was called barren. For with God nothing will be impossible." Then Mary said, "Behold the maidservant of the Lord! Let it be to me according to your word." And the angel departed from her (Luke 1:34–38).

As with Zacharias, the angel used the word "will" a number of times. That which was impossible would come to pass. This miracle would take place. The miracle child would be a male. His name would be Jesus. He would be great, the Son of the Highest, and He would inherit the throne of His ancestor King David. He would reign over the House of Jacob, and His kingdom would be everlasting. It would be eternal. Forever.

But notice Mary's reaction to this incredible news. At face value, her reaction was similar to that of Zacharias. However, she wasn't struck dumb for unbelief. This is because she asked in faith (see verse 45.) She didn't doubt God in the slightest. He said it would happen, so it would surely come to pass.

If you or I search through the Scriptures with a proud and skeptical spirit, we will come up with nothing but dry bones. There will be no life in them. Reading the Bible without trust is like reading a book in the dark. Faith is a light, and the life will go out of any marriage if one spouse loses faith in the other. This is the case with human relationships, and also the case with God (see Hebrews 11:6).

Those who ask in faith hear from God. He resists the proud skeptic and gives grace to the humble seeker of truth. They that seek do find. Those who knock do have the door opened for them. If you are not seeking God, you need to. You and I are sinners and we desperately need a Savior. If you don't believe that, that's your problem. Unbelief. It's a killer.

"How shall I know this? For I am an old man, and my wife is well advanced in years." — Zacharias, blinded by an angel. "How can this be, since I do not know a man?" — Mary, blessed by an angel. I thought for sure someone would have mentioned this earlier. I don't see any difference between the way Zacharias is questioning the angel and the way Mary questions the angel. They both ask the same question: How? They both provide reasons for their question. Because I am an old man and my wife is old, too; because I do not know a man. Yet Zacharias was blinded while Mary received a reasonable explanation. Why the special treatment?

That "special treatment" is called "grace." That's where God gives unmerited favor. It's unearned and undeserved. But didn't Mary earn God's grace by having a humble heart? No, then it wouldn't be unmerited. It was that Mary's humble attitude made a way for her to receive the grace of God. Think of a wicked criminal. If a judge wants to show him mercy, what does he look for? He looks for humility and contrition (sorrow for his crime). The judge then gives him mercy. He says, "I can see that you are sorry for what you did. Had you been proud and arrogant, I would have thrown the book at you, but your humble heart allowed me to show you mercy. You are free to go." The criminal didn't earn mercy (an oxymoron). He simply made mercy possible.

It is God's grace that saves sinners from death and Hell. Look closely at the wording of Ephesians 2:8–9: "For by grace you have been saved through faith, and that not of yourselves; it is the gift of God, not of works, lest anyone should boast." It is grace alone that saves us through the medium of faith (trust). It is a gift (gifts can't be earned). It is "not of yourselves." It's "not of works." It is truly unmerited favor. So when you read the Scriptures, feel free to ask questions, but do it with a humble heart, otherwise you stand on your own oxygen hose.

> *In Mark 14:62, in response to the chief priests and the council who have posed the question "are you the Christ," Jesus says: "I am. And YOU will SEE me sitting at the right hand of power, and COMING with the clouds of heaven." Did those men SEE him coming with the clouds or sitting in power? They almost certainly saw him die, but the Bible never confirms that this prophecy was fulfilled. In fact, when the Bible record ends, his disciples are still awaiting His coming. It never happened. It still hasn't happened 2,000 years later. Why, Ray? Is Jesus a false prophet?*

Some eschatological positions would say that Jesus knew this chief priest would still be alive when the judgment of the Jewish people took place in A.D. 70. "Coming with the clouds of heaven" was an Old Testament imagery of an army decimating a place (Ezekiel 30:3–4, 38:8–12; Deuteronomy 33:26–27; Jeremiah 4:13; etc.). Jesus, in the context of the temple also affirmed this imagery in Matthew 24. Some would say Revelation 1:7 indicates that "they who pierced him" would include this high priest. Jesus proved that He was in power (Matthew 28:18) and controlled the most powerful nation the earth had ever seen to do His bidding, which was to punish Israel for their sin like previous generations: but this time it was for the rejection and crucifixion of Jesus (violating the first and fifth commandments).

Also, you forgot that the hour is coming when all that are in their graves shall hear His voice (see John 5:28). There is going to be a resurrection of the just and the unjust (ee John 5:29). *Every* eye will see Him. The chief priests will bow the knee before Him. So will Hitler and every murderer, rapist, thief, and liar. Richard Dawkins will bow down to Jesus Christ as Lord of the universe and Creator of all things (see Romans 14:11; Philippians 2:10). By Him everything was created (see Colossians 1:16), and every human being will see Him in His glory, including you. John saw the resurrected Christ and trembled in terror. He shines with a brightness above that of the sun (see Acts 26:13).

So it would be wise to stop asking whether He was a false prophet. Instead, confess and forsake your sins, and put your trust in Him while He extends His mercy to sinful men and women. He has waited for 2,000 years because He is not willing that any perish, but that all come to repentance. Everything Jesus said would happen has happened throughout history (see Matthew 24 and Luke 21), and you can therefore bet your very soul that those men who Jesus said would see His coming will see it.

I invite you to compare the genealogy in Matthew 1:1–17 to the genealogy in Luke 3:23–28. They are remarkably incompatible, and one wonders how you can call the Bible, in this case, anything but utter confusion. Perhaps, though, you can answer a question I've had for a long time. How can Jesus be the son of Joseph, as both these genealogies attest? Wasn't God his father? Aren't these genealogies, in fact, entirely pointless? And isn't the prophecy that the Messiah would descend from the line of David thus unfulfilled?

Study the wording in Luke 3:23 closely. It says "as was supposed" or "what was thought to be the son of Joseph." He wasn't. He was the Son of God (God manifest in human form). Then carefully look at the wording of Matthew 1:16. It says, "Joseph the husband of Mary." In neither case is Joseph called the father of Jesus.

In both of these cases, the genealogy goes through the lineage of David (see Luke 3:31 and Matthew 1:6). There is no confusion at all in these lists. If names in both don't reconcile, there are rational explanations. For example, in Matthew we are told that "Jacob begat Joseph," but Luke 3:23 says, "Joseph, the son of Heli." Luke's record was "according to Law" (a literal translation of "so it was thought" in Luke 3:23), indicating that Joseph was not actually the son of Heli but was reckoned his son according to the law. Joseph was the son-in-law of Heli, Mary's father.

Please don't get your information from atheist websites. They hold up the same old mistaken arguments, and they never seek an answer. Imagine if you reject God's gift of everlasting life and end up being justly punished for your sins, solely because you believed what some stranger said on an atheist website, instead of sincerely looking into it yourself. What a tragedy.

A skeptic wrote: "But I don't believe that Ray's 'vile worm theology' is the consistent teaching of the Bible, nor is it consistent with a healthy self-image. Here are instances, in fact, where certain people are considered 'blameless': 'This man [Job] was blameless and upright; he feared God and shunned evil' (Job 1:1). 'But I lead a blameless life; redeem me and be merciful to me' (Psalm 26:11). 'Both of them [Zechariah and Elisabeth] were upright in the sight of God, observing all the Lord's commandments and regulations blamelessly' (Luke 1:6). We don't see this universal groveling in the muck over one's imperfection. We can thank the Church for that miserable sentiment."

It's important to understand that when the Bible speaks of someone being "blameless" it doesn't mean that they are without sin. It simply means (in the Old Testament) that they trusted in God through animal sacrifice and were therefore released from the condemnation of His law. It was God's mercy that saved them, looking forward to the Cross in the same way that we look back to the Cross.

This is also the legal state of the Christian (in the New Testament). He is a wicked sinner like every other human being, but because of the sacrifice of the Lamb of God, he is counted as blameless. The law of God has no demands on him. He is "justified" in the sight of God.

The word translated "blameless" [Greek *amomos*] is used a number of times in the New Testament:

> That you may become blameless and harmless, children of God without fault in the midst of a crooked and perverse generation, among whom you shine as lights in the world (Philippians 2:15).

> (God) chose us in him before the foundation of the world, that we should be holy and without blame before Him in love (Ephesians 1:4).

> Christ . . . gave himself up for [the church] . . . to present her to himself as a radiant church, without stain or wrinkle or any other blemish, but holy and blameless (Ephesians 5:25–27;NIV, see also Revelation 14:5).

This is an incredible truth of the Bible. All who repent and trust alone in Jesus Christ will be found blameless on the Day of Judgment. That means that God's law will not condemn them to Hell.

That's why it doesn't faze me when I am accused of being a liar and a hypocrite by atheists. God's approval is all that matters. If I am a liar and a hypocrite (a pretender) I will end up in Hell, but if I am genuine, I will be found blameless.

Look at this wonderful promise for every Christian: "Who shall bring a charge against God's elect? It is God who justifies. Who is he who condemns? It is Christ who died, and furthermore is also risen, who is even at the right hand of God, who also makes intercession for us" (Romans 8:33–34).

The Bible says to stone people to death. It is an archaic book that has no relevance to modern society.

If you are found guilty of murder in the United States, there is a possibility that you will be executed by means of the electric chair. Authorities will forcefully take you, strap you to an electric chair, and switch on the power. Have you ever seen photos or read accounts from eyewitnesses as to what happens to someone who dies that way? Have you seen photos of what happens to their eyes and their tongues? The person is literally cooked, and it doesn't happen quickly. Often things don't go as planned. After seeing photos of victims, if I had a choice between being stoned or the electric chair, I would choose stoning. Both are horrific, but the thought of capital punishment by *any* means is strong incentive for me to never take the life of another person through murder.

Ray, in light of the following verses: "The world also shall be stable, that it be not moved" (1 Chronicles 16:30); "The world also is stablished, that it cannot be moved" (Psalm 93:1); "The world also shall be established that it shall not be moved" (Psalm 96:10); "Who laid the foundations of the earth, that it should not be removed for ever" (Psalm 104:5; kjv), are you willing to admit the Bible is in error, or does the earth in fact sit immobile and fixed in the sky?

The above question is typical of the skeptic. He reads those verses and somehow comes up with the thought that the Bible is saying that the earth sits "immobile" and "fixed in the sky." No doubt this comes from a list of so-called contradictions and mistakes in the Bible on some atheist website. But where does it say that the earth sits *immobile* in the sky?

Skeptics love to twist Scripture just a little to make their point. They clutch at the weak straws of metaphors or figures of speech to try and prove that the Bible says that the sun revolves around the earth, etc.

So let's look closely at what the above verses actually say: "He has fixed the earth firm, *immovable*." "Thou hast fixed the earth *immovable*." "He has fixed the earth firm, *immovable*." The Bible says that the earth is *immovable*. It cannot be *moved*. So now is your chance to prove your point. Run outside and *move* the earth. Perhaps you and your friends could jump on it, or find a rocky outcrop and push it together. Maybe after that little experiment you will concede that the earth is immovable. So is Scripture. You can push, twist, pull, and jump on different verses, but the Word of God isn't going to move. It is a rock. It cannot be broken. It will judge you on the last day (see John 12:48). You only twist it to your own destruction (see 2 Peter 3:16).

Chapter Three

Science: Scientific Thought and Evolution

It is abundantly clear that, while bringing up the "Darwin is Racist" gem again, Ray has not bothered to read one word of any actual science text, let alone The Origin of Species. *Yet he is still convinced he can accurately summarize evolutionary theory.*

When I read *The Origin of Species* I was impressed with Charles Darwin. If he were alive today I am sure that he would quickly rise to the top of Disney's imagineers, or earn big bucks as a Hollywood screenwriter for science fiction movies. It must also be noted that Darwin's racist beliefs are most clearly pronounced in his *Descent of Man* and his letters.

Among fantastic speculations, Darwin noted that black bears swam for hours with their mouths open, catching insects in the water. He believed that if they kept their mouths open all day, every day (for a long period of time), that they would acquire "larger and larger mouths, until a creature was produced as monstrous as a whale."[24]

Those who take the time to read *The Origin of Species* can read his own explanation as to why there is no empirical evidence for his model — that all "intermediate varieties" have disappeared — just like the Mormon's golden plates that Jesus supposedly gave to Joseph Smith. There's one big difference, though, between the golden plates and the intermediate varieties. The Mormons say that only two golden plates are missing. Darwin says that *millions* of fossils (what he referred to as "innumerable") are missing. After 150 years of searching, the missing links are still missing.

According to Darwin, the giraffe's tail evolved because it needed it to swish away flies. Think of how many millions of years the poor animal had to put up with those pesky flies before the tail evolved so that it could do its work. They can also read how Darwin wondered if the vulture became bald (over millions of years) because it kept putting its head into rotting meat. But he advised caution because "the head of the clean-feeding turkey is also naked."[25] You may also notice that millions of men are bald, and hopefully doubt that it's because their ancestors rubbed their foreheads into rotting meat.

In Darwin's book, nothing is as God created it. God didn't create the giraffe with a tail to swish away flies. Neither did He create the vulture or turkey with a bald head. Instead, all of creation miraculously evolved — from the bear's mouth to the giraffe's tail, and for some reason it has all reached the point of maturity during our lifetime, and (after millions of years of redundancy) now functions as it was intended. Move over, J.R.R. Tolkien, Arthur C.

Clark, and J.K. Rowling. These three combined don't hold a candle to Charles Darwin. Most of their fans know their writings are fantasy. Darwin's faithful followers don't.

Evolution has evidence to back it up. It's not perfect and not complete but it is more compelling than believing in magic. Are you afraid to look at the evidence? I could link to some starter information on my neglected blog if you aren't afraid of it.

A simple-minded man once maintained that the story of Pinocchio was true. A wooden doll did become a human being. He not only believed that it was true, but he maintained that he had evidence to back it up. He said that its proof was that there was such a thing as a wooden doll of the type spoken of in the story, and that it has been also proven that there was once a child that looked like that doll. Therefore, in his mind, that was evidence that the wooden doll came to life. He didn't see the disconnect between the two thoughts.

Then he said that his theory was scientific and he was intelligent, and anyone who didn't believe as he believed was unintelligent and unscientific. Yet everyone knew that non-life cannot become life. (This is a law of biology called the law of biogenesis.)

Such describes the modern atheist. He has an adamant belief that there's no evidence that there is any God or gods, and yet he himself is part of life. He believes that non-life produced life, and he doesn't see the disconnect. Then he tries to justify his belief by embracing the wild speculation of evolution, the idea that he believes is "not complete but is more compelling than believing in magic."

I have practiced magic for many years, and have watched the astounded expressions of thousands of people whose eyes were easily fooled by my hands. Prestidigitation has taught me that human beings are extremely gullible, and never has there been such mass gullibility as in the case of those who believe in evolution *without compelling evidence*. For them, a bump on a whale bone becomes positive proof that whales had legs, or some amino acid means that chickens were once dinosaurs. Obscure non-transitional fossils become attestation that humans are actually primates. This is the conviction of the simple-minded, who believe anything that paleontologists and professors pontificate.

No doubt the argument will continue between those who love God and those who don't. But I have looked at the "evidence" for evolution, and I don't believe their strange interpretations as they do. I am not afraid of their "starter information" because their "finish" doesn't exist.

Instead, the evidence is backed up by the power of the Creator, who promises to reveal Himself to those who obey Him (see John 14:21). There is no greater evidence for truth. When God reveals Himself to any human being, the argument is over.

The lowly appendix, long-regarded as a useless evolutionary artifact, won newfound respect two years ago when researchers at Duke University Medical Center proposed that it actually serves a critical function. The appendix, they said, is a safe haven where good bacteria could hang out until they were needed to repopulate the gut after a nasty case of diarrhea, for example. . . . "Maybe it's time to correct the textbooks," says William Parker, Ph.D., assistant professor of surgical sciences at Duke and the senior author of the study.[26]

What an interesting way to admit that the theory was wrong. Again. For years we have heard the argument that the appendix was positive proof for evolution, and that those who didn't accept the evidence were unscientific knuckleheads.

Suddenly it goes from being a useless evolutionary leftover to being something that "serves a critical function." There's no apology. There's no admittance of wrong. They discovered that God made it for a reason, and all we get is, "Maybe it's time to correct the textbooks." Maybe? Of course it won't be. Why should it, when the entire foundation for evolution is founded on the same sort of fiction?

Of course, believers will parrot that there's no need for an apology because science is never "wrong." Rather, it's forever seeking the truth but it can never be sure that it has found it. So it has license for recurrent falsehood. When it comes down to it, those who have faith in evolution can never have the assurance that what they are believing is true and trustworthy. It is Darwinian quicksilver.

However, I'm not concerned if someone wants to believe in a fairy tale. That's their business. What concerns me is if their belief conflicts with the truth of Christianity and that causes them to reject the gospel. Then it becomes a matter of great concern because it becomes a stumbling block for their eternal salvation, and that's a tragedy beyond words.

A Christian wrote: Atheist Challenge: 1. Put frog in blender; 2. blend frog; 3. put blender on kitchen table; 4. wait for frog to hop back out. Should be a no-brainer for evolution — given that we know for sure everything required to make a living frog is present. Don't hold your breath!

An atheist responded. "That frog is dead. It took billions of years for complex life to evolve on earth. I suppose, theoretically, if I took the frog's remains and placed them on an alien world with conditions similar to early earth something might arise after another few billion years, but I can't say for sure."

The atheist obviously doesn't know what atheistic evolution believes. It believes that in the beginning there were no frog "remains" and no "conditions" for life. There was no dried frog skin, frog bones, no blood, kidneys, liver, eyes, ears, nervous system, and heart. In the beginning there was no frog nor genes nor DNA. No frog. There was nothing. Nothing at all. There was no air, no water, no sunlight. Nothing.

That's what atheistic evolution believers believe. Now pull back and give that some objective thought. Forget about the hypocrisy and established religion and those "dumb old Christians" with their unscientific beliefs and their 6,000-year-old earth. Just think about how the atheist believes that for some reason nothing created everything — frogs (male and female), water (with a perfect consistency to maintain life), air (with its perfect mixture of gases to maintain life), sunlight (to maintain life), oxygen-giving trees, beautiful flowers, masses of birds, succulent fruits, the seasons, etc. There were no atoms, no molecules, no genes, no bacteria. There was nothing.

As if that's not insane enough, when an atheist wants to hold onto his belief that nothing caused all this to happen billions of years ago, he then predictably says, "Then who made God, if He was the initial cause?" In his unthinking mind, his unbelievable belief then becomes rational because he refuses to accept the eternality of God.

It doesn't take much effort to expose those lies, for one, on his first "observation" of lacking evidence (or as he prefers to keep repeating ad nauseum, things that cannot be answered), on how the sexes evolved. (Obviously, Mr. Comfort is blissfully ignorant of certain organisms that are hermaphrodites, or asexual.) He might have gotten the slightest of clues by visiting a common reference site such as Wikipedia.

Why, how, and when did evolution produce both male and female in the 1.4 million species that are on the earth? I am forever being accused of being all sorts of unrepeatable names for my willful ignorance in not believing the explanation given to me by evolutionists. They often point to the same source and say that all I need do is read it and I will understand how evolution works when it comes to the evolving of the sexes. However, the explanation is a masterpiece of how to confuse simply by diversion, commonly known as "verbal sleight-of-hand." Here is a sample from their source, followed by my answer:

> In all sexual species, the population consists of two sexes, only one of which is capable of bearing young (with the exception of simultaneous hermaphrodites). In an asexual species, each member of the population is capable of bearing young. This implies that an asexual population has an intrinsic capacity to grow more rapidly each generation. The cost was first described in mathematical terms by John Maynard Smith. He imagined an asexual mutant arising in a sexual population, half of which comprises males that cannot themselves produce offspring. With female-only offspring, the asexual lineage doubles its representation in the population each generation, all else being equal.

My answer:

> Wait a minute! In his imaging, he has just pulled a big rabbit out of the hat. He is talking about asexuality and suddenly makes reference to "males" and "female-only offspring." But there's no explanation as to where he and she came from, or why, or how he and she came, or how long

it took for him and her to evolve. Where *did* she and he come from, and, just a minor point to the evolutionist, why did he and she also appear in the 1.4 million of the earth's species?[27]

So there you have it. There's actually no explanation at all, just a supposition that "evolution did it." Magic. Male and female suddenly appeared. If you are a believer you will be impressed. I'm not. Not in the "sleightest."

"You believe nothing created something or the Creator created something? It's a simple question." Yes, indeed it is. It is also a simple presupposition offered as a limited hypothetical "choice," excluding as it does any number of other possibilities, all of which are probably beyond our current knowledge.

Many times I have been called a liar because I have said that an atheist is someone who believes "nothing created everything," which of course is a scientific impossibility. This is a huge embarrassment to the atheist. Instead of being seen as an intellectual, such a thought reveals him to be a fool, just as the Bible says (see Psalm 14:1).

Professor Richard Dawkins isn't embarrassed to say that he believes that "nothing created everything." This is what he said in his book *The Ancestor's Tale: A Pilgrimage to the Dawn of Evolution*:

> The fact that life evolved out of nearly nothing, some 10 billion years after the universe *evolved literally out of nothing* — is a fact so staggering that I would be mad to attempt words to do it justice"[28] (italics added).

He's right, of course, about someone being mad if they even attempted to explain it.

But those who believe it need not attempt the madness of trying to explain it or justify it. If they want to hold onto the label "atheist" and still think that they are intellectual, they can pretend that there is another alternative. All they need to do is employ the evolutionist's popular "language of speculation" by using the word "probably," and then hope that the answer is "beyond our current knowledge" — they enroll in the "Don't Understand How" club (DUH).

How true is Scripture when it says of the atheist: "Although they knew God, they did not glorify Him as God, nor were thankful, but became futile in their thoughts, and their foolish hearts were darkened. Professing to be wise, they became fools" (Romans 1:21–22).

Ray: This has been asked before, by myself and others, but once more for the record: What evidence would convince you to seriously reconsider your views on evolution?

You are right about my being asked this before, so I will try to make this as clear as I possibly can, so you and others will know where I stand and not have to waste your time asking again.

I think that evolution is the most unscientific, faith-based, fundamentally brainless idea that ever had the misfortune to come out of a human mind. To compare it to true science is a joke. There is nothing even slightly scientific about it.

When I read *The Origin of Species* (page after laborious page), it was like reading the ravings of a man who truly believed that the sun was square, that it came out at night, and that it was made of ice.

The closest thing to truth that Charles Darwin ever said was when he admitted to someone (in *Origin of Species*) that a cold shudder came over him because he thought that he may have devoted his life to a fantasy. He certainly did. But that in itself isn't amazing. What is utterly amazing is that so many *believe* the unbelievable fantasy. For me to believe every impossible miracle and weird thing that happened in the Bible is completely effortless, compared to the wild speculations that the average evolution believer swallows without question. And what's the magic word that makes the fantasy come true? Time. Lots of it. I can hardly believe that anyone could believe what evolutionists believe, and what's more — no one could ever begin to convince me to believe what they believe; not in a million years.

Look at the intellectual embarrassment of where it leads. Richard Dawkins says we are related to turnips: "It is the plain truth that we are cousins of chimpanzees, somewhat more distant cousins of monkeys, more distant cousins still of aardvarks and manatees, yet more distant cousins of bananas and turnips."[29] Let's get this straight. Dawkins mocks me for believing that the banana was "designed," *and yet he believes it was his cousin!* Evolution is the greatest joke on earth, and the professor is laughing all the way to the bank with the money of naïve believers who swallow his banana and turnip crazy talk.

Besides all this, I know God personally, experientially, and intimately — the One atheists don't believe exists. He is the One who said, "Let there be light," created every animal as male and female, caused them to bring forth after their own kind, and made man in His own image, not as some primordial bacteria.

In case I haven't made my point clear, let me summarize. You would have infinitely more chance of convincing me that the sun doesn't shine, that water isn't wet, and that God didn't make little green apples than you have of convincing me of your childish fantasy.

If the word "bigot" comes to mind to describe me, so be it. I have no choice in the matter. It's either common sense or absolute foolishness. (I choose common sense, and if I'm wrong, I lose nothing at all. If you are wrong, you lose everything.)

Your letters-to-words analogy breaks down because it assumes that earth was somehow the end result of fine tuning, when in reality God could have just created an earth without all this unnecessary and rather pointless matter out there. That would have been better evidence to me that God had intentions for our planet. . . . I don't understand why God would do things that way if He was trying to communicate that He is a good designer who had explicit intentions for the human race. Grrr, I'm not sure how to communicate this right. This will work for now.

I carefully read everything you wrote. Your "I don't understand why God would do things that way if He was trying to communicate that He is a good designer who had explicit intentions for the human race" is the predictable conclusion for anyone who rejects Genesis 1 and 2. You don't believe that we live in a "fallen" creation that is in chaos — killer earthquakes, tornados, hurricanes, thousands of diseases, suffering, pain, and ultimately death for all of us (the results of the Fall are much more comprehensive). In so doing, you stand on your own oxygen hose.

What if I said, "I don't believe you exist. There's no evidence. The huge comment I found on this blog that had your supposed name on it was the result of random chance that appeared from nothing and came from no one. On top of that, I think I am intelligent for having such a belief."

Such crazy talk would be more than foolish. It would be a horrible insult to you.

And God created humans with an appendix because . . . ?

The reason for the question is the old and misguided thought that evolutionists have that the appendix is vestigial, and that therefore it is just one more proof that evolution is true. In Charles Darwin's *On the Origin of Species* (1859) and in his later works, he referred to several "vestiges" in human anatomy that were left over from the course of evolution. These vestigial organs, Darwin argued, are evidence of evolution and represent a function that was once necessary for survival, but over time that function became either diminished or nonexistent. So here is the answer to the question from two different sources. One is Christian, the other is secular:

1. "However, as doctors learned more about these organs, especially the appendix, they discovered that they are not useless after all. The appendix is a small pouch that extends off the large intestine. It also is called the vermiform (worm-shaped) appendix because it looks like a three-inch earthworm. In recent years, doctors have observed that the appendix is a tough soldier against infection, especially in people who have been exposed to some types of radiation. Inside the appendix is lymphoid (LIMfoid) tissue which helps produce white blood cells that fight disease. Also, early in a child's life the appendix is relatively larger than it is in adults. It is during these early stages of life that the appendix appears to play an even bigger role in guarding the body from infection."[30]

2. *Scientific American* said, "For years, the appendix was credited with very little physiological function. We now know, however, that the appendix serves an important role in the fetus and in young adults. Endocrine cells

appear in the appendix of the human fetus at around the 11th week of development. These endocrine cells of the fetal appendix have been shown to produce various biogenic amines and peptide hormones, compounds that assist with various biological control (homeostatic) mechanisms. There had been little prior evidence of this or any other role of the appendix in animal research, because the appendix does not exist in domestic mammals."[31]

I am amazed that evolution believers would attempt to grasp at such weak straws when the winds of truth have already blown them away.

. . . Because the appendix does not exist in domestic mammals. It doesn't? And I thought it was a rather prominent structure in herbivore animals. What about the tailbone or third molars, Ray?

It's really not a "tail" bone. It is the bottom of your backbone, and without it you couldn't go to the bathroom each day. It supports the necessary muscles.

Claims that wisdom teeth (third molars) usually cause damaging crowding have not held up under the scrutiny of recent empirical studies.[32] Wisdom teeth were given by God for you to chew and enjoy your food. Be wise and take care of them. Floss.

Atheists do not believe the universe is a "creation" in the sense you use the word. Thus they cannot believe it was "created." Most of those answering, such as myself, just think the universe was formed due to natural causes. Natural causes, properties, phenomena are not a creator.

I can understand why atheists do not believe that the universe was "created," or even that it's a "creation." Both those words speak of a Creator, so you need to find another word that doesn't have that connotation. I noted that you are careful not to say that the universe is eternal. That would be a way out, but you know that such a belief is a scientific impossibility (e.g., all the heat should have been used up). Time would have caused an eternal universe to disappear into dust eons ago. So the natural word to settle on, when it comes to what happened in the beginning, is to say that the universe "formed." An atheist is someone who believes that everything formed itself.

So if there was such a thing as an atheist Old Testament, it should begin with "In the beginning there was nothing, and nothing formed itself into everything." But you can't believe that because of what you have said. You believe that nature existed, and that nature ("natural causes") formed itself into everything. But if nature existed, then you don't have a beginning. What caused nature?

There's a huge elephant in the room and it's standing on your foot. You are trying your best to deny its existence and yet still sound educated. I feel your pain.

I'll let it slide that the bulk of elements which comprise the human body are primarily found in the air, not the soil (carbon, hydrogen, and oxygen). But Ray, are you honestly affirming the case that all the ingredients to produce life were present on earth before life existed?

Definitely not. Dirt is just dirt. It has no life at all. The life came from the source of all life — God: "And the Lord God formed man of the dust of the ground, and breathed into his nostrils the breath of life; and man became a living being" (Genesis 2:7).

You are a living being. Your life is invisible (your soul). When that soul leaves the body in which it lives, no one will see it leave. Your doctor may just say, "This man is now dead," but he won't see your life pass into eternity. He will make that assessment because your life has left your body. Again, God is the source of that life. When people become Christians they are "born" of the Spirit of God (see John 3:3–5). The Holy Spirit abides in them — they receive the life of God.

If you carefully study the words of Jesus, you will notice that He continually made the incredible claim that He was the very source of life: "I am the way, the truth, and the life" (John 14:6), "I am the resurrection and the life" (John 11:25), "I have come that they may have life" (John 10:10), etc. The Bible says of Him: "In Him was life" (John 1:4), "Christ who is our life" (Colossians 3:4), and "He who has the Son has life" (1 John 5:12).

So when you reject Jesus Christ, you are rejecting the most valuable thing in the universe: life. And why do you reject eternal life? Because you love your sin. See John 3:19–20 for details.

It was eminent scientist Stephen Hawking who said, "There have been various ideas, but for me the most attractive is that the universe was spontaneously created out of absolutely nothing."[33] So it's not too difficult to take that a step further and believe that it was *God* who spontaneously created the heavens and the earth.

But the Book of Genesis goes on to tell us that God then made man from the soil of the earth. Such a thought seems a scientific impossibility. However, according to Yale University, the elements that make up the soil are as follows:

1. potassium
2. calcium
3. magnesium
4. phosphorous

5. iron

6. manganese

If God made the human body from the soil, it makes sense that both the soil and the body would be made up of the same elements. Let's then see if these six elements that are present in the soil are also in the human body:

1. Potassium: "Potassium plays an important role in smooth muscular and cellular functioning, cardiovascular functioning, muscle contractions, nerve transmission, in conversion of glucose into glycogen and muscle building, etc."[34]

2. Calcium: "Calcium comes in many forms, and is a whitish substance which is a primary ingredient in things such as chalk, ivory, pearls, and bones. It is known as the fifth most common element in the earth's crust and is a primary mineral in the human body."[35]

3. Magnesium: "Magnesium is essential to the functioning of the human body because it transmits nerve impulses, causes the contraction of muscles, and is integral to healthy development of teeth and bones."[36]

4. Phosphorous: "Phosphorus is present in bones and teeth and combines with calcium to form calcium phosphate which is the substance which gives the skeleton rigidity. It is also present in every cell in the human body and in the body fluids as well."[37]

5. Iron: "Iron is a mineral found in every cell of the body. Iron is considered an essential mineral because it is needed to make part of blood cells."[38]

6. Manganese: "Manganese is an essential element to the human body."[39]

Is it then a coincidence that the same six elements that are in the soil are also in the human body? That's what you have to figure out before death takes you into eternity . . . when your body decomposes and turns back to the soil, from which it came (Genesis 3:19).

The following plea appeared on www.liveScience.com beneath an article called the "Top 10 Missing Links."

First, let me confirm that I am not a creationist, nor any other religionist. I am not biased in any way whatsoever. I am just a "seeker of the truth." Secondly, I'm new to this "leave a comment" thing and this will be the third time I've left a comment, so I'm hoping it will be "third time lucky" and I get a response.

I've asked this question regarding "evolution" and specifically about the human "intermediary" fossil evidence, including ANY unequivocal, supporting "evidence" of the "common ancestors," hundreds of times and, no doubt, you've been asked it even more times, but I've never been given the precise information I've requested. Instead, I have been swamped with mountains of ambiguous, contrary, and contradictory websites and links, ALL of which are unfairly balanced, or biased in favor of evolution. I have spent months on end sifting through this information, and sometimes I do come across what I think is the "needle in the hay stack," but it ALWAYS turns out that, despite the author's assurance, the proving evidence is too weak and controversial and requires "blind faith" of those who are prepared to accept it as valid evidence of evolution.

So, for what I hope is the "final" time, my question/ request is, "IS there ANY positive, UNEQUIVOCAL, human, 'mediatory' fossil evidence available (out of what should be at least half of the fossils found) including any of the 'common ancestor' (and, actually, what kind of creature the common ancestor was and what name has been given to it)?" If your answer is a resounding "YES," then could you PLEASE give me the precise location and names of that evidence (avoiding "Lucy" and her equally strongly refuted "friends," of course!). Thanking you in anticipation.

The answer given:

> If I understand correctly . . . you're expecting evidence of a "missing link" or of the ancestor to all modern primates. There is no "missing link" because the evolution of humans is a branched tree with many extinct species. We are the current hominids living. Neanderthals were a different species that briefly lived alongside ours; we did not evolve from them as many people incorrectly think. Some of the "missing" information you seek regarding ancestry can be found in DNA. I suggest you stop searching the Net for good info and buy a book. Carl Zimmer has some great ones such as *Smithsonian Intimate Guide to Human Origins and Evolution: The Triumph of an Idea.* The "needles in the haystack" are out there and being discovered, but it sounds like you're not looking in the right places and maybe not sure what you are actually looking for. Evolution is happening all the time; just look at things like bacteria, plants, and insects. But you can think of breeding as a similar process (like all those miniature dogs), but it is a result of human interference and not nature, but gene related all the same and that's what we're talking about with evolution. Check out those books I mentioned. There's no blind faith

involved in evolution . . . just evidence, and as in all sciences, more being discovered every day.[40]

This person *pleaded* for evidence "specifically about the human 'intermediary' fossil evidence, including ANY unequivocal, supporting 'evidence' of the 'common ancestors.' " What did he get? "There are no missing links. Go read a book and study bacteria, plants, and insects." The dilemma is that there are no undisputed species-to-species transitional forms.

I don't believe in evolution. I simply have confidence in science.

When I watched a documentary on the discovery of "Ardi," the famous fossil that was touted as a missing link, I was amazed that the discoverers didn't date the bones at 4.4 million years old. They instead dated the soil in which they were found. My immediate thought was, *How do they know that Ardi's age was the same as what they perceive as the soil's age, and how do we know that the dating system is accurate?* Let's say I die next week and I'm buried in soil that geologists say is 2.6 million years old. One hundred thousand years pass and new geologists dig up my bones. They want to know how old my bones are, but instead of testing them, they test the compacted rock strata in which I was buried and conclude that they are 2.6 million years old.

I tried looking up the details regarding Ardi's age of 4.4 million years and all I could find was that they looked at the volcanic layer above and below. This makes me skeptical because I know that in dating Lucy they had to drive miles away from the site to even find anything they could measure, dating wise. Was the dating done at the site where Ardi was found? If not, or if we don't know, are we just taking their word for it?"

Thanks to an honest atheist, the cat came out of the bag. He said, "Strictly speaking, you'd be taking geologists' word for it."[41] And therein he revealed the blind, unquestioning faith of the average believer in evolution.

Evolution has been proven despite what your idiot homeskool "textbooks" told you. The only questions are about the details.

Those who are homeschooled usually excel at spelling (it would seem that you weren't homeschooled).

I have met many kids who have been educated by their parents (using "idiot" homeschool textbooks), and I have found that they are consistently respectful, well-adjusted to life, sociable with their peers, and extremely knowledgeable. This is because those who are educating them deeply love them, and they have the ability to care for them as individuals. Studies have shown that children whose parents are directly involved in their education are more apt to excel in academics. In addition to this, extended periods of time together strengthen family relationships, not only between the child and his parents but also with his siblings.

Granted, by not being educated by the public system, their kids will miss out on learning how to communicate using filthy language. They will also likely miss out on the use of illegal drugs. According to a survey by the National Center on Addiction and Substance Abuse at Columbia University, "Millions of U.S. teens attend 'drug-infested schools' where students routinely see drugs used, sold, or kept on schools grounds. . . . Thirty-one percent of high school students — more than 4 million — see drug dealing, illegal drug use, or students high or drunk at least once a week on their school grounds."[42]

Homeschooled kids are more likely to miss out on sexual promiscuity, contracting sexually transmitted diseases (one in four

U.S. females has a sexually transmitted disease),[43] being bullied, and maybe being shot to death (to date, there have been shootings resulting in the deaths of students in 76 different U.S. public schools). According to the National Conference of State Legislatures, an incredible one in five kids in public schools have seriously considered suicide: "19.3 percent of high school students have seriously considered killing themselves."[44]

Back in 2007, nearly 6.2 million students in the United States between the ages of 16 and 24 dropped out. According to ABC, "A study this week from Strong American Schools reports that 40 percent of seniors still do not understand the math they were taught in the eighth grade. And an earlier study from Common Core found that nearly a quarter cannot identify Adolph Hitler, more than half cannot place the American Civil War in the right century, and a third do not know that the Bill of Rights guarantees free speech."[45] The American public school system is a failure.

Had homeschoolers attended public school they would have also been brainwashed by an unproven myth about human origins and ended up believing that they are nothing but an animal with no ultimate moral accountability. Evolution doesn't simply teach that we have a common ancestor in primates. It seriously teaches that we *are* primates,[46] and if the result of public schooling education is to reject God and His gift of eternal life, the depth of that tragedy will only be measured in the light of eternity.

Sadly, millions of impressionable young people have already been brainwashed into believing that evolution is a proven fact and that all it lacks is "details." How could any theory be proven when there are no details to provide proof? The missing link (the details) is still missing. All evolution believers have is a blind faith in what they have been taught by other believers in that idea, and "evolution did it" isn't good science. It's a pseudo-science. And that's a fact.

If you want to maintain that atheists truly do believe "nothing created everything" (which we don't, but you don't care about that, do you?), then it absolutely does follow that you yourself believe that "nothing created God," who then proceeded to create everything else. If you want to claim that God always existed, then I will do exactly the same thing with the universe. This is what you do, Ray. You dismiss the scientific explanation as "impossible" or "ridiculous," and then use the very same explanation when asked about your God. It's pathetic, Ray. You're pathetic.

And in doing so you reveal that you don't understand the basics of science. The second law of thermodynamics shows that the universe cannot be eternal because it would have crumbled into dust (in time).

The fact that I'm pathetic doesn't change the fact that either you believe that nothing created this universe or you believe that something created it. You have no fence to sit upon. Either you are an atheist (believing that nothing created everything) and, as the Bible so aptly says, are a "fool" (see Psalm 14:1), or you believe that something created it and are therefore not an atheist.

If it were a scientific explanation, it shold be repeatable . . . and big bang isn't.

When did life appear on the earth? Was it billions of years ago, or was it something like 6,000 years ago? The Smithsonian doesn't know. They use the word "probably" when it comes to when life began, which is probably the most-used word when it comes to the theory of evolution. I use the word "probably" when it comes to it being the number-one word, because I really don't know. I could be wrong.

Imagine stepping into a plane that you believed was "probably" safe, or into an elevator that has cables that are "probably" secure. But think of what the evolution believer does. He believes that earth *probably* began billions of years ago, and therefore wholeheartedly rejects the Bible's account of creation and consequently its offer of Heaven and warning of Hell. All because of probably.

The word "know" is used 717 times in the Bible (KJV), but you won't find the word "probably" even once. That's because when God says something, His promise is immutable. You can have faith in it, believe it, rely on it, cling to it, and completely trust it with all of your heart, mind, soul, and strength. I have been doing that for over 37 years and never once have I been even slightly disappointed.

It's because of this absolute trust in God that I know that I have everlasting life. I know that my many sins are forgiven, and I know that I have escaped the damnation of Hell.

This implicit trust is something that God gives to all those who repent and trust in Jesus. If we call upon His name He gives us a new heart with new desires, "seals" us with His Holy Spirit, imputes what is called "righteousness" to us, and on top of that He gives us the ability to trust Him and His promises in such an unshakeable way.

I know that many of you say that you don't believe that God exists (let alone have faith in His promises), and of course you don't have faith in what I have to say because you think I am a lying, money-hungry, snake-oil salesman. But I will say it anyway: I cannot find words in the English language to express my love for God. I am at a loss for words when it comes to my fathomless appreciation, my burning gratitude, my exploding thankfulness — for the fact that He has saved me from the power of the grave and given me everlasting life.

Write us off if you will, but you cannot take that reality from those who love God. It's ours forever . . . and all you have is "probably."

DNA isn't proof of God's existence. There's no code-maker because it's not a "code," it's simply a molecule.

It was Francis Crick who discovered DNA and received the Nobel prize for his amazing work. Look at his own wording from the lecture he gave on October 11, 1962:

> Part of the work covered by the Nobel citation, that on the structure and replication of DNA, has been described by Wilkins in his Nobel Lecture this year. . . . I shall discuss here the present state of a related problem in information transfer in living material — that of the genetic code — which has long interested me, and on which my colleagues and I, among many others, have recently been doing some experimental work.[47]

The discoverer of DNA called it "information transfer" and a genetic "code."

Richard Dawkins, in his book _The Blind Watchmaker_, said:

> Every single one of more than a trillion cells in the body contains about a thousand times as much precisely coded digital information as my entire computer. . . . Each nucleus, as we shall see in chapter 5, contains a digitally coded database larger, in information content, than all 30 volumes of the Encyclopedia Britannica put together. And this figure is for each cell, not all the cells of a body put together.[48]

DNA is a complete code, a plan, intricate information for a living organism. Chance does not produce intelligent information.

Considering that God made the world and the universe in six days and considering He created Adam in about 4004 B.C., why is it that scientists say that the most distant planets are over 20,000 light years away? This means that the light from these planets has been traveling in space for 20,000 years, far longer than the universe has existed even if you count a day of creation as 1,000 years.

I have no idea of the exact date that God created the universe or when He created man, but via genealogic studies we know it is fairly close to 6,000 years ago. However, I believe that Adam was made as a mature male, with fully developed and working eyes, strong muscles, a full-size heart, robust lungs, and eight pints of life-giving blood. In other words, the first man was created in a state of adulthood with an appearance of age. To the casual observer, the ten-minute-old Adam may have looked like a 30-year-old man.

Another thought is that when God created the Garden of Eden, He made it with beautiful trees. Ten minutes after He created it, a casual observer may have looked at the tall trees and understandably estimated that they were 30 or 40 years old, when in truth they had only existed for ten minutes. It would be the same case with a rock a geologist may have picked up minutes after creation. Scientifically speaking, he may understandably have estimated that it is thousands or even millions of years of age, when in truth it had just been created by God.

If God had the ability to speak the sun into existence, He also had the ability to cause its light to instantly shine upon the earth.

The Bible doesn't say, "And God said, 'Let there be light,' and there were four minutes of darkness as the light from the sun traveled 93 million miles to the earth . . . and there was light." It would seem that the very instant God spoke light into existence, it was manifest. So it's very easy for me to reconcile the Scriptures with the findings of science.

When atheists argue about the existence of God, they forget that someone who has been born again knows God. So there is no argument about His existence for those who know Him. You may as well write to me day after day telling me that my wife doesn't exist. I could give you her background history, but because I know and love her, every argument you raise about her non-existence is senseless and meaningless.

The fact of Sue's reality has no bearing at all on you or the way you live your life. But if you deny God's existence, the fruit of that willful ignorance is that you will live your life without reference to His requirements. That will be to your eternal detriment, and that horrifies me beyond words.

> *It seems much more likely that a number of small changes over the course of millions of years led to the complexity we see today. If not, how do you explain things like the blind spot in the human eye? The fact that our urinary tract runs through the prostate? The tail all embryos have and some babies are born with? The fact that we breathe and eat through the same hole? None of those make sense in light of special creation, but they do make sense when you actually understand the processes of evolution.*

Why doesn't it make sense from a creation standpoint? The design works rather well. Furthermore, I must point out the language of speculation that you are forced to use in your opening sentence. Words like "seems" and "likely" are always present when a Darwinian believer speaks of what he believes. Let's address your issues. I don't have a blind spot in my eye. Both of them see very well and I am thankful for the 137 million light sensitive cells that make sight possible. Do you have a blind spot in your eye? If you do, I suggest that you see an eye doctor and see if he can either fix it or get you another eye.

You may detect a little sarcasm, which I think is thoroughly justified. To think that a camera lens could create itself is insane, but to believe that the human eyes, and the eyes in 1.4 million different species, created themselves is off the charts.

The prostate wraps around the tube that carries urine out of your bladder. If you think evolution caused the prostrate to wrap around the tube, and you think it's a poor design, then you have a problem with the designing mind of evolution.

As far as I know, all mammal embryos have backbones that are dubbed "tails." The embryo has to end somewhere. Leaves have tail endings, dogs have tails, and Darwin had the biggest tale of all, and you believed him, so now you think we came from fish. But the ending of the embryo isn't vestigial, and neither is the "tail" bone in human beings. Without it you wouldn't be able to go to the bathroom each day because the muscles that make it possible would have nothing with which to connect.

Finally, to breathing. The next time you have a bad cold and your nose is really stuffed up, take a moment to thank God that He gave you another opening that allows you to breathe. Then use that opening to confess your sins, forsake them, and then trust in the Savior so that you will be forgiven on the Day of Judgment.

> *There are hundreds of thousands of transitional fossils that prove that evolution is true. You don't know what a transitional fossil is.*

There are millions of transitional forms in the fossil record. Millions. However, there are *no kind-to-kind* transitional forms (e.g., amoebas to cows). Transitional forms are evidence of God's creation. Kind-to-kind transitional forms are evidence of Darwinian evolution of which there are none. That's what's missing from Darwinian evolution — *kind-to-kind* transitional forms. There's no scientific evidence of *kind-to-kind* transitional forms in the fossil record. None. I have repeated my point in the hope that you and your friends get it. Evolution is based on faith. You believe what you have been told. You believe Darwin, you believe your professor, you believe carbon dating, and you believe the pseudo science of evolution. It's all based on faith. Most believers of evolution will believe anything, as long as it's not in the Bible.

> *Ray, please show us how you plan to falsify the following evidence for the fact of evolution:*
>
> *Protein functional redundancy, DNA functional redundancy, transposons, redundant pseudogenes, endogenous retroviruses, anatomical parahomology, molecular parahomology, anatomical convergence, molecular convergence, anatomical suboptimal function, molecular suboptimal function, nested hierarchies, convergence of independent phylogenies.*
>
> *Transitional forms: reptile-birds, reptile-mammals, ape-humans, legged whales, legged seacows, chronology of common ancestors,*
>
> *Anatomical vestiges including: atavisms, whales and dolphins with hindlimbs, humans tails, molecular vestiges, ontogeny and*

developmental biology, mammalian ear bones, reptilian jaws, pharyngeal pouches, branchial arches, snake embryos with legs, embryonic human tail, marsupial eggshell and caruncle, present biogeography,

Past biogeography of: marsupials, horses, apes, and humans.

You certainly are a believer! I'm not. I don't have a belief in evolution. Can't you just accept that? I don't have any belief in evolution because all this "evidence" isn't evidence at all, but rather *interpreations* of evidence. When looking at the actual evidence, we interpret it based on God's Word, not a humanistic religion.

Take for example your "humans tails." I don't believe (as you do) that I'm an ape, and I don't have a "tail bone." Neither do you. It's called the "coccyx vertebrae" and it has an important function. It's not a leftover from evolution. It holds the muscles that help you go to the bathroom. You would be in big trouble without it. It is not vestigial as you have been told.

Neither is the appendix. The appendix is part of the body's immune system. It's not vestigial as you've been told.

I'm sorry, but I don't have time to go through your whole cut and paste list. Giving me a list like this is like me giving you a list of the Bible's 66 books and saying that each one is proof for the existence of God. And when you don't study every book and come back at me with an answer for each, I declare myself the winner.

There are no winners and losers with the evolution and creation argument. If you are right and there's no God, then there's no afterlife and you won't get to even say, "I told you so." You don't win.

If I'm right and there is a God and Hell exists, then (because you have violated the law of God) you will be justly damned. I don't "win" if that happens. The thought horrifies me. Please, come to your senses, confess and forsake your sins, and trust in Jesus Christ.

The Christian says, "I obviously can't speak for Ray but I can say this: Any and all portions of the theory of evolution are ridiculous. Stop believing in this fairly tale for grownups." Do you deny that, e.g., one species of fruit fly (e.g., Drosophilia melanogaster) can evolve into another sort of fruit fly (e.g., Drosophilia paulistorum)?

Most believers in the theory are confused between what is called "micro-evolution" (changes within "kinds" — differing types of dogs, cats, insects, etc., which isn't evolution at all), and Darwinian evolution, for which there is no undisputed empirical evidence. In your case, the *Drosophilia melanogaster* fruit fly that "evolved" into a *Drosophilia paulistorum*, is still a fruit fly. No "evolution" has taken place. Big words only impress small-minded people. No "kind" has evolved into another "kind." There's no imperial evidence for it happening in the creation around us, or in the historical fossil record. Everything rather is as the Bible so clearly presents it — animals beginning as male and female and every kind bringing forth after its own kind. If you are a believer in evolution, you are basing your eternity on a childish fairy tale that has nothing to do with science.

Evolution proves that there is no need for God's existence.

Ed Blyth, a creationist, described the process of natural selection more than 25 years before Darwin. Darwin gave that process the name "natural selection." Darwin, as well as Alfred Russel Wallace, tried to use this as the mechanism for evolution. The modern definition of natural selection is "a process in nature in which organisms possessing certain genotypic characteristics that make them better adjusted to an environment tend to survive, reproduce, increase in number or frequency, and therefore are able to transmit and perpetuate their essential genotypic qualities to succeeding generations."

This "natural selection" can be seen throughout creation, as different plants adapt to soil conditions or to climate, or animals adapt because of predators or because of selective interbreeding.

However, every animal that adapts always stays within its own kind. Cats don't breed and become another kind of animal. No animal is transformed into another "kind." This is often referred to as "micro evolution" — a small change that happens within a certain "kind" of animal. Birds remain birds, animals remain animals, and plants remain plants. Micro-evolution and macro-evolution are not the same thing. Macro-evolution is unobserved and moving in the opposite direction as micro. Macro is often viewed as molecules-to-man evolution.

Darwin was anguished over what he saw in natural selection. He spoke of it as "the clumsy, wasteful, blundering, low and horridly cruel works of nature."[49] It *is* a cruel work of nature when a painful disease kills the weakest of children (three of Darwin's children died before they reached adulthood), or a weak and innocent deer is devoured by a stronger, vicious predator.

The Book of Genesis explains this terrible state of nature as a "fallen" creation that is filled with disease, death, and decay. The Book of Romans also addresses the "cruel works" of fallen nature by calling it "slavery to corruption" and saying that "the whole creation groaneth and travaileth in pain together" (Romans 8:21–22; KJV).

However, those who reject the Genesis account of the Fall end up in an ocean without a rudder. They are blown about by the many winds of speculation. After addressing the truth of micro-evolution, Darwin makes the speculation that perhaps (like plants and animals) mankind also adapted, over a great deal of time, and natural selection took him from primitive primate to human.

The problem with his model is that nowhere in the entire creation do we see natural selection take one kind and change it into another kind. Neither is there evidence of any *kind-to-kind* transitional forms in the fossil record. Every animal brings forth after its own kind, just as it is stated in the Genesis account.

Not only was Darwin's leap of speculation completely unscientific, there were other serious difficulties. Alfred Russel Wallace, the co-discoverer of modern evolutionary thought, declared that natural selection could not account for humanity's intellectual and moral abilities.[50] Why then was such unscientific conjecture so embraced by so many?

When *On the Origin of Species* was first published, English biologist Thomas Henry Huxley said that it was a "veritable Whitworth gun in the armory of liberalism,"[51] and though he wasn't convinced about natural selection, he proceeded to position himself as "Darwin's bulldog." Think of it. Even though Huxley didn't believe the idea, he backed it and said that it was a massive weapon that promised freedom. Freedom from what? Belief in evolution promised mankind liberty from any ultimate moral responsibility to God. That belief got rid of sin, the Fall, and, most of all, man's accountability to his Maker.

According to Douglas Futuyma, professor of evolutionary biology at the State University of New York, "Darwin's (and Wallace's) concept of natural selection made this 'argument from design' completely superfluous . . . it provided a purely natural explanation for order and the appearance of design."[52] In other words, evolution paved the way for atheism.

As one commentator said, "Darwinism is also ferociously savage — the weeds die out, the fittest survive, there is no moral universe because all is pre-programmed and we have no free choice."[53] The die-hard Darwinist believes that there is no moral universe. Such is the tragic delusion of the theory of evolution.

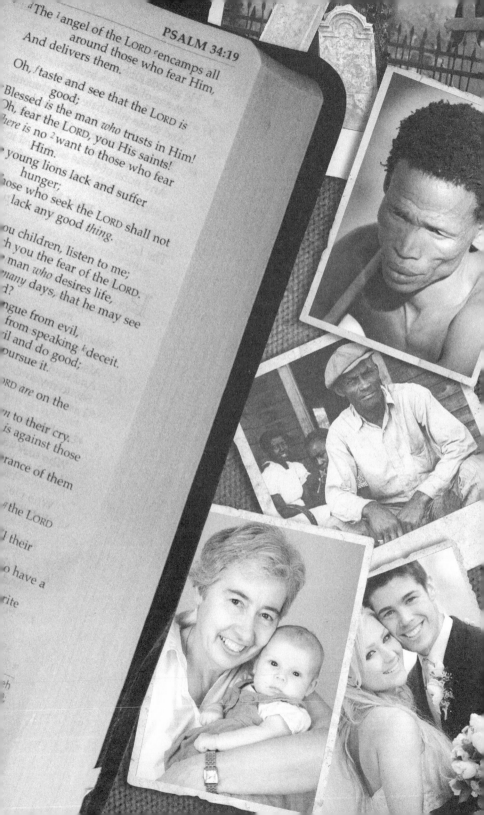

The ¹angel of the LORD ᵉencamps all
around those who fear Him,
And delivers them.

Oh, ᶠtaste and see that the LORD is
good;
Blessed is the man who trusts in Him!
Oh, fear the LORD, you His saints!
There is no ²want to those who fear
Him.

young lions lack and suffer
hunger;
those who seek the LORD shall not
lack any good thing.

you children, listen to me;
ᵍ you the fear of the LORD.
man who desires life,
many days, that he may see
d?

ngue from evil,
from speaking ᵏdeceit.
il and do good;
oursue it.

RD are on the

n to their cry.
is against those

rance of them

the LORD

their

o have a

rite

Chapter Four

Philosophy: Beliefs and Worldviews

I understand that you don't need "proof" to believe in your God or any god for that matter, but you would think that if all these fantastic stories were even almost true there would be proof all over the place or at least even something that is reasonable proof.

You may be able to believe without proof (embracing the theory of evolution), but I can't. I need evidence to evaluate. I wouldn't bother dedicating my entire life to a cause if there was no proof.

The primary proof for me is knowing God, and that comes from God's Word. Before my conversion on April 25, 1972, at 1:30 a.m., I knew that God existed via creation (Romans 1). You can't have a creation without a Creator. That's impossible. Modern atheists say that there is no "creation." But then they have to rid themselves of the word "made," because that also speaks to a Maker. Try to think of something that was made that didn't have a maker. Clothing and shoes usually have a label on them so that you can know the identity of the maker. Cars also have a label. Even if the Mercedes company didn't have "Mercedes" on their vehicles, common sense will tell you that the car had a maker. Its design denotes a designer. It was "design" that convinced Einstein that God existed, even though he didn't believe that God is "personal."

As for all the fantastic stories, there is evidence for many of them, if you care to look. The problem is that you no doubt have presuppositions, so there's not much point in looking. Which takes me back to the primary proof. Go through the test in www.needGod.com. That will show you that you need a Savior. Then read John 14:21 a few times. It's either true or it isn't.

When you come to know God, everything else falls into place. It's like sitting in a dark room believing that it is empty. Someone says to switch on the light. Once you do that, you will see everything from a different perspective.

Charles Darwin was a humble genius, and a good man who cared about others, whereas the Bible is filled with dangerous myths.

I once believed that Charles Darwin wasn't a racist (as some suggested), and that even if he was, his personal morality was irrelevant when it came to the theory of evolution. But after studying him closely, I changed my mind. Let's look at his own words:

> At some future period, not very distant as measured by centuries, the civilized races of man will almost certainly

exterminate and replace throughout the world the savage races. At the same time the anthropomorphous apes, as Professor Schaaffhausen has remarked, will no doubt be exterminated. The break will then be rendered wider, for it will intervene between man in a more civilized state, as we may hope, than the Caucasian, and some ape as low as a baboon, instead of as at present between the negro or Australian and the gorilla.[54]

While the above quote seems as nebulous as one of the prophecies of Nostradamus, close study reveals Darwin's point. He is predicting that civilized races would replace savage races. The gap between savages and the civilized races would become wider, like the gap he saw between the white races and the ape. That means that there would no longer be a closeness, such as the one he saw between the negro and the gorilla.

He was saying that Blacks were closer to gorillas than the whites were. Who could deny that this is a blatantly racist statement, particularly when contemporary society says that just saying or even putting the "N" word in print is racism? Yet modern admirers of Darwin try to justify his racism by saying that he loved the Negro, and that he spoke kindly of their intelligence. He wrote during his voyage on the Beagle, "I never saw anything more intelligent than the Negros, especially the Negro or Mulatto children."[55]

After reading *Life with a Black Regiment,* Darwin wrote to the author to thank him "heartily for the very great pleasure" which it gave him: "I always thought well of the Negroes, from the little which I have seen of them; and I have been delighted to have my vague impressions confirmed, and their character and mental powers so ably discussed." He despised proponents of slavery, referring to them as "the polished savages in England," while saying of a black lieutenant that he'd never met anywhere "a more civil and obliging man."[56]

Charles Darwin believed that the black race was closer to the gorilla than the white race, but he thought that they were friendly, well-behaved, and intelligent. His attitude was similar to that of a man who likes well-trained dogs. He thinks that they are friendly, well-behaved, and some are extremely intelligent.

His racism was blatant, indefensible, and was shaped by his belief in evolution. It's interesting that a number of atheists have agreed with me in my belief that Darwin was a racist. They said, "I feel no compelling need to justify Charles Darwin's racism," and, "Why do you assume that Darwin's racism was shaped by his belief in evolution? The man lived at a time when blacks in many western nations were still owned as chattels, when creationist anthropologists freely speculated that the different races were separately created species (a view Darwin undertook to refute). The idea of races arranged on a ladder from 'lowest' to 'highest' (generally with one's own subgroup on top) was commonplace among creationists of his day." And, "Of course Darwin was racist, he lived in a society in which racism was the norm. . . ."

However, after much research, I do concede that you won't find anything in Darwin's writings that would indicate that he in any way felt blacks were to be treated as inferior or that his views of them were due to their skin color. *He just thought that they were closer to gorillas than whites.* Imagine if you said *that* on prime-time TV. You would stir up a hornet's nest. Then imagine trying to justify your belief by saying that you despise slavery and that you think black people are intelligent and friendly. You could also add that your convictions that they are closer to gorillas than whites has nothing to do with skin color.

James D. Watson, the evolutionary scientist and author of *Darwin: The Indelible Stamp: The Evolution of an Idea* got himself into very hot water back in 2007. According to the Associated Press, "The Independent newspaper put Watson on its front page, against the words: 'Africans are less intelligent than Westerners, says DNA pioneer.' "[57] The *London Times* reported, "One of the world's most respected scientists is embroiled in an extraordinary row after claiming that black people are less intelligent than white people. James Watson, a Nobel Prize–winner for his part in discovering the structure of DNA, has provoked outrage with his comments, made ahead of his arrival in Britain today."[58]

Like Darwin, Watson's belief had nothing to nothing to do with skin color. He said that we should not discriminate on the basis of color, because "there are many people of color who are very talented, but don't promote them when they haven't succeeded at the lower level."[59] He just thought that white people are more intelligent than blacks. For that, he was labeled a blatant racist by many in contemporary society.

So, if I am right and Charles Darwin was a racist by today's standards, why not simply accept it and move on? Why did so many resort to name-calling?

"You deserve the worse that a Hell could provide. . . .
I truly despise you, Ray."

"Ray, you are nothing but a deceitful snake oil salesman."

"I truly find you detestable."

"You are disgusting, Ray. A disgusting inhuman wretch."

"Ray, I can't state enough how much of a pitiful little rat you are. You are a coward of the highest order."

"You should go back to your home country and convert some stupid people there."

"No! We don't want him back!"

"You stink."

In a debate, when your opponent falls back on childish name-calling, it reveals that he is feeling frustrated because he is losing the argument. I can understand why so many feel that way. I have never hidden my agenda. All I want is for people to doubt evolution enough to re-examine the claims of the gospel. This is because I believe that there's nothing more important than where you will spend eternity.

What do Darwin's personal views on race have to do with our modern understanding of evolution? Nothing. Absolutely nothing, Ray. Even a fool knows this.

Indeed, Darwin's racism has nothing to do with the *credibility* of his idea of evolution. It should stand or fall on its own merits. However, the model itself teaches that all men are not created equal. Darwinian evolution doesn't say that human beings are made in the image of God and endowed by their Creator with certain unalienable rights. It rather states that they are mere animals, some closer to apes than others. It opens wide the door to racism. And remember, Darwin expected non-Caucasians to be exterminated, and people like Hitler took him at his word.

An article entitled "Americans Still Linking Blacks to Apes" on scienceblog.com presented the findings of research done by psychologists at Stanford, Pennsylvania State University, and the University of California–Berkeley. Co-author of the study Jennifer

Eberhardt said, "It's a legacy of our past that the endpoint of evolution is a white man. . . . I don't think it's intentional, but when people learn about human evolution, they walk away with a notion that people of African descent are closer to apes than people of European descent." I wonder where they get that notion from?

I've asked this several times and never received an answer. What is the name of the person who brought you to Christ? Who convinced you to trust in Jesus? You never have answered me. Why is that?

The name of the person who led me to Christ was Graham Reid. He was a New Zealand surfing buddy in a group of five or six close friends. I befriended him when I was newly married and decided to go on a two-day surfing trip (in April of 1972) with the group. I didn't know that Graham was a Christian. All I knew was that he was a nice guy who didn't cuss and had a Bible in his car.

During the first night of the trip, I read Matthew 5:27–28 and realized that I had sinned against God. Later that night Graham shared the good news of the gospel with me — that Jesus suffered in my place to save me from my sin and the reality of Hell. At 1:30 a.m. I was born again and came to know God.

The rest of that weekend he kept repeating the words, "Ray Comfort a Christian. I don't believe it. I don't believe it!" The reason for his being astounded was that he knew that I was incredibly happy. I was 22 years old with my own prospering business, my own home, a lovely wife, and the freedom to slap "GONE SURFING" on the door of my surf shop whenever I felt like it. What more could I want? But he didn't know that I was *desperately* seeking truth. I didn't know why I was alive. I could see that the whole of humanity is marking time until death swallowed us. Life didn't make sense.

One night I wept as I looked at my beautiful wife and realized that death could take her in a heartbeat. With tears streaming down my cheeks, I cried, "Why! Why?" I didn't think that anyone heard me that dark night, but I was heard, and my cry was answered six months later when I fell at the Savior's feet.

I will be forever thankful for the night that my faithful friend took the time to share the gospel with me:

> "I sought the LORD and He heard me, and delivered me from all my fears" (Psalm 34:4).

> *"Who are we? We find that we live on an insignificant planet of a humdrum star lost in a galaxy tucked away in some forgotten corner of a universe in which there are far more galaxies than people."*[60] *Carl Sagan*

God knows what Carl Sagan did in the last days or even last minutes of his life. Cancer has a way of stopping us in our tracks and making us think about life's bigger issues. However, at the time Carl Sagan wrote the above, it showed how "lost" he was. He believed that we live on a lost planet, forgotten by whoever ("whatever" cannot forget) created it. But he was misinformed.

We are not at all insignificant. The fact that this earth has oxygen, that it has water, that it is just the right distance from the star we call the sun sets us apart as having great significance. Neither are we at all "forgotten" by God. True, the number of galaxies is innumerable, but each one of us is intimately remembered by our Creator. He knew us before we were formed in the womb, He knows how many hairs are on our heads, and He even knows our thoughts before we think them. Of course you don't believe that if you are an atheist, but that doesn't change its truth.

Imagine the tragedy and sense of betrayal — if you base your whole life on the empty philosophy of Carl Sagan, and find on Judgment Day that he did repent and trust the Savior. Imagine seeing him separated to Heaven, and yourself cast into Hell because you followed him in life but weren't privy to his death.

I think it would be wise not to follow the vain philosophy of any man or woman (Colossians 2:8). Rather, follow Jesus Christ. He is the way, the truth, and the life. How do you do that? Call upon His name. Do it today. Simply humble yourself, repent of your sins, and put your trust in the Savior — and you will know the truth, and the truth will make you free (see John 8:31–32).

You cannot disqualify scientific endeavors [the way you do] unless you truly understand it. Since it is obvious that you have no idea, you should rather shut it. Try and learn what the whole paleontology, geology, and biology are about, how the evidence is collected and analyzed, then come back and tell those things with a straight face.

I will let the wisdom of Charles Spurgeon address the subject of "science" in his day:

> Away from the old-fashioned belief of our forefathers because of the supposed discoveries of science. What is science? The method by which man tries to conceal his ignorance. It should not be so, but so it is. You are not to be dogmatical in theology, my brethren, it is wicked; but for scientific men, it is the correct thing. You are never to assert anything very strongly; but scientists may boldly assert what they cannot prove, and may demand a faith far more credulous than any we possess.

Forsooth, you and I are to take our Bibles, and shape and mould our belief according to the ever-shifting teachings of so-called scientific men. What folly is this! Why, the march of science, falsely so-called, through the world, may be traced by exploded fallacies and abandoned theories. Former explorers, once adored, are now ridiculed; the continual exposure of false hypotheses is a matter of universal notoriety. You may tell where the learned have encamped by the debris left behind of suppositions and theories as plentiful as broken bottles. As the quacks, who ruled the world of medicine in one age, are the scorn of the next, so has it been, and so will it be, with your atheistical savants and pretenders to science. . . .

So the bubbles go on bursting, and meanwhile more are being blown, and we are expected to believe in whatever comes, and wait with open mouth to see what comes next. But we shall not just yet fall down and worship the image of human wisdom, notwithstanding all the flutes, harps, sackbuts, psalteries, dulcimers, weekly papers, quarterly reviews, and boastful professors. Show us a man of science worthy of the name, and then we will not follow him if he dares to oppose revealed truth; but show us one in whom the next generation will believe; at present, there is not one alive worthy to be compared with Newton and other master-minds reverent to the Scriptures, compared with whom these men are mere pretenders.[61]

In what ways do you experience divine wrath and mercy? I'm not asking for a sermon or a collection of Bible verses but rather a testimony of your experience.

I have not experienced divine wrath, although the night of my conversion I was well aware of it. Think of a wanted criminal. He has committed multiple and serious crimes. One night, he is stealing in the dark of a moonless night. The darkness gives him a sense of security. Suddenly police spotlights flood the area. He is exposed. The darkness is no longer a cover for his unlawful activity. He hears a loud voice tell him that ten sharpshooters have his pounding heart in their sights. One wrong move and he is a dead man. At this point, he has a choice. He can try and make a run for it and die, or he can lift his hands high in surrender and live.

Before I was a Christian, I was engaged in serious unlawful activity, even though I hadn't violated man's law. I was unaware that God saw my thought-life and that I had violated His perfect Law — the Ten Commandments. The night of my conversion was when the light came like a flood. My many sins were exposed. The darkness was no longer my security. The loud voice of my conscience told me that those Ten Commandments, like ten great cannons, had my pounding heart in their sights. If I tried to run, I knew that God's law would justly send me to Hell. At that point I had a choice. I could run from the light, or I could lift my hands high and surrender. On the 25th of April, 1972, at 1:30 a.m., I surrendered.

Guilty though I was, I found that the Judge of the universe was rich in mercy. He dismissed my case because Jesus Christ had paid my fine in His life's blood two thousand years ago, then He granted me the gift of everlasting life. If you have ever seen the movie *Ben-Hur,* at the conclusion you will hear a wide-eyed Judah Ben-Hur say, "I felt His words take the sword out of my hand." That's what happens the moment you surrender the weapons of your hostility.

Ray, if my kid gets sick should I take him to the doctors? Or would that be interfering with the work of your God in his life?

It was the wisdom of Solomon that said that a merry heart does good "like medicine" (see Proverbs 17:22). So medicines are good.

Here's what we would do when our kids were young and became sick. We would pray for them and take them to the doctor if it was more than a minor complaint. If the doctor saw fit to put him in the hospital, we would pray even more — that God would give wisdom to the doctors, because hospitals can be very dangerous places. Around 40,000 people die on roads in the United States each year. However, a massive 200,000 people die in hospitals because of medical mistakes and infections. That means that in ten years, two million people die while in the care of our medical professionals. That's frightening.

One way to keep out of hospitals is to control the appetite (see Proverbs 23:2) and cultivate the virtue of self-control (see 2 Peter 1:5–7). Many serious complications and terrible diseases that result in untimely death are a result of obesity. An incredible 58 million Americans are overweight, while 40 million are obese, and 3 million morbidly obese. No wonder our health care system is overloaded.

By the way, obesity is not caused by genetics as some maintain. Neither is it a disease (although some medical conditions cause weight gain). When the Americans liberated those who were in concentration camps in 1945, there were no obese people. They were *all* skinny. Obesity is caused by self-indulgence — by eating too much food or by eating the wrong food. A good rule to live by for healthy living is: "If God created it (vegetables, fruit, etc.), eat it. If man has messed with it, read the label, carefully."

Another key to staying out of hospitals is to realize that you should cleanse yourself (particularly your hands) under running water to keep free from diseases. This is what the Bible instructed the Jews to do thousands of years before science discovered its importance (see Leviticus 15:13). It's God's instruction book on how to live this life, and how to get to the next. Don't ignore it.

I've tried praying, and it doesn't work!

I wonder what you would think of the mentality of someone who said, "Some time ago I e-mailed the White House and told the president that he needed to be at my house last Friday, with a gift for me. He didn't show up, so I believe that he doesn't exist." I'm sure you would think that your friend was either naïve or mentally challenged.

If you have ever prayed for something and felt that your prayer didn't get past the ceiling, you are probably right. Just as there is a certain procedure that you must go through to have an audience with the president, so there are certain procedures that you must go through to have an audience with God.

Here's some information that may help you. The first thing to understand is that, by our nature, we are enemies of God, and that His wrath abides on us (see John 3:36). We are rebels. So the odds of getting an audience are stacked against us. The Bible tells us that our sins have made a separation between God and us, so that He will not hear us (see Isaiah 59:1–2). He resists the proud but gives grace to the humble. So stop clicking your fingers and expecting God to come running like some sort of divine butler. It doesn't work that way (see James 4:3–4). Instead, humble yourself, repent, and trust the Savior. That will give you direct access (see John 14:6).

Then make sure you understand that God always responds to prayer. That way you will never be disappointed. Sometimes He says yes and grants our desires. Sometimes He says no and doesn't. Other times He makes us wait so that we learn to exercise faith and patience.

Most people don't understand that there are two types of the will of God. There's His *permissive* will, where He will allow things to happen to the Christian. These may not seem to be beneficial for us, but God promises to work them out for our good, in the light of eternity.

Then there is the *perfect* will of God. Such revelations are very clear in Scripture. You can go to the bank on them. Actually, I take that back. Banks nowadays aren't that reliable. Let's just say that when you see a promise in Scripture that is clearly God's absolute will, you can rely on it. Completely. For example: "Whoever believes in Him should not perish but have everlasting life" (John 3:16).

Ray, are you afraid of dying?

This is perhaps the shortest question I've been asked, but I will probably give it one of my longest answers, because it's a question with which every sane person wrestles. So I will be thoughtful and very candid with my answer.

The quick response is "Yes, I am fearful," and "No, I'm not." I am not afraid of dying, but I am afraid of the *process* of dying (as I have noted that a number of atheists have also said).

On December 5, 2009, I turned 60 years old. That's more than six decades of life. When I turned 20, I was shocked. It took me by surprise. I loved being a carefree teenager, and it was suddenly gone. When I turned 40, I was quietly horrified. People who were 40 were "middle-aged." They were balding, potbellied, and it seemed to me that they were past the exciting adventure of life. But when I turned 60, I was quietly philosophical. I'd had time to give this one much deep thought.

There are some good things about getting old. Sue and I can enjoy those good old black and white movies again and again, for the first time. There is also the blessing of being around to turn 60. I have friends that didn't even make it to 50. One was killed in a bus accident. It rolled on him. Another drowned in shallow water when he hit his head on a rock. Another was killed in a plane accident. Others were taken by cancer. Most of us know someone whom cancer took in their youth, or someone who died tragically in a car accident.

When the Beatles sang "When I'm 64," I'm sure they never thought that two of them wouldn't make it to 64. The "when" never came. One went quickly with a bullet; the other, slowly with cancer. Every year 40,000 unfortunate Americans are killed on the roads, around 18,000 are murdered, and hundreds of thousands die of cancer and other terrible diseases.

Then there are those who die in warfare. Millions have been cut off in their twenties by a bullet or a bomb, and the majority of those didn't even experience the joy of having kids, let alone growing old.

That's my short list of good things I can think of about the twilight years. Now for the long list of bad things.

I am very aware that when one turns 60, one enters the decade of loss. I will lose any youthful looks that I have left. Any muscle strength I have now will quickly diminish. My skin will become loose and lifeless. My eyesight will go. So will my hearing, thought process, memory, and taste buds. My immune system will weaken and make me vulnerable to a stack of terrible terminal diseases.

These depressing things happen to everyone, despite regular exercise, daily juicing, and consuming a careful diet. No one can beat this rap. All this and much more will come in the next 20 years, if death doesn't come to me first through a heart attack or aneurism or 101 other unexpected surprises.

So "the process of dying" isn't a matter of a few weeks on a hospital deathbed. It happens over 20 or so years.

In one of Spielberg's memorable movies (if my memory is to be trusted), the aging process happened to one evil character in an instant of time. He had to choose the cup from which Jesus drank at the Last Supper (the Holy Grail). He believed that if he drank from it, he would live forever. He quickly grabbed the most attractive golden cup and began to drink. He wasn't perceptive enough to realize that Jesus was a lowly carpenter and would have had a simple and humble wooden cup. The moment he took it to his lips, he aged from a healthy 40-year-old — to 100 years — to a dry and dusty skeleton that crumpled to the ground.

The immediate outlook in life for *any* of us (even for the most optimistic of positive thinkers and health-conscious juice drinkers — whether a Christian or an atheist) is pretty gloomy.

So am I afraid of this process of dying? Part of the answer is that I'm about as afraid as a faithful soldier who is going into a battle from which he is certain he will not return. His is a natural and understandable human emotion, because he loves life and deeply values those he loves. Only a shallow-thinking person would have no fear.

But here now is the most important and exciting part of my answer. Almost every skeptic makes a huge mistake when it comes to the issue of faith. He thinks that a Christian is someone who believes in the existence of God despite an overwhelming lack of evidence. That's why he chooses to be an unbeliever. He never seems to be able to differentiate between *intellectual faith* and *implicit trust.*

Let's say I step into an elevator on the 84th floor of a massive high-rise. I have just entrusted my life to it. Any apprehension I have will be in proportion to the trust I exercise. If I have no trust in the elevator, I will have a ton of fear. If I have absolute trust, I will have no fear at all. The ingredient that makes the difference between the two states of mind is knowledge. If I have knowledge that the elevator is state-of-the-art, computer operated, checked daily, and I *believe* that knowledge, my trust will grow.

But if I *personally* inspect the 12 three-inch-thick unbreakable steel cables that hold each elevator, my trust will grow more. If I understand that the computer system has a backup and immediately shuts down the elevator and calls inspectors at the first hint of trouble, my trust will grow even greater. The more trust I have, the less room there will be for fear to plague me.

However, if I *choose* not to believe what I am shown about the computer system, the cables, the inspections, etc., I will be left to be plagued with my fears. My trust in the elevator is a choice, based on knowledge that is simply believed. Remember, that knowledge I have is more than a belief that the elevator exists.

So when it comes to the issue of God and salvation, the diehard skeptic disqualifies himself before he even begins. By choice he refuses to intellectually believe that God exists, despite the overwhelming evidence of creation and the moral nature of the God-given conscience.

So if you truly believe that God doesn't exist (which I doubt), you may as well stop reading at this point, because you are in the category of what the Bible calls "unreasonable." But for the *reasonable* skeptic who understands that his existence is indeed hopeless (in the truest sense of the word), there is a wonderful hope. So please stay with me. Just keep in mind that it is essential to make sure you understand that the trust a Christian has in God is *not* the belief that He exists.

Here's how the trusting Christian deals with his fear of death. He has knowledge that God *cannot* lie. He knows that He is morally perfect. That means that He is without sin. As the Scriptures say, "In Him is no darkness at all" (1 John 1:5). The 18-mile-thick unbreakable titanium cables of His promises are absolutely worthy of the Christian's trust. There is no doubt of that. The believer *knows* the reality of the verse "He who promised is faithful" (Hebrews 10:23). When fear comes, it cannot get past this knowledge, and that results in trust. Such trust comes as a gift at the point of conversion. It is part of the new birth of John chapter 3.

The more the Christian trusts the promises of God, the less fear he has. The two are incompatible. That means that the trusting Christian can say with the Apostle Paul, "I know whom I have *believed* and am *persuaded* that He is able to keep what I have committed to Him [my life] until that Day [Judgment Day]" (2 Timothy 1:12, italics added). He is saved from death and the just deserts of his sin.

That leaves the faithless skeptic alone with his fears. He has refused knowledge of the faithfulness of God, so he is left with certain tormenting uncertainties. Often his pride will not permit him to admit that he has any fears, but they will come. He doesn't realize that "fear *involves torment*" as the Bible says (1 John 4:18, emphasis added). He has forgotten what it is like to wake up after a terrifying nightmare. Sometimes it takes about ten minutes after waking up just to shake off such gripping fears. And when it comes to the subject of trust in God, the unbeliever has no power to stop fear from gripping his very soul to the core, because he refused the antidote of faith.

The seed of fear torments with a question. It whispers, "What if?" *What if* Jesus spoke the truth and God does consider lust to be adultery? *What if* He does see hatred of one's brother as murder? *What if* He has seen and remembered every single secret sin and every sinful imagination of the heart? *What if* Hell does exist? *What if* that "silly little anti-science, money-hungry, lying, stealing, fanatical, banana-man idiot-preacher" was actually speaking the truth?

Millions know what it is to be paralyzed by a tormenting fear. It drives them to insanity, to drink, and it even drives many to suicide to escape its torment. If you are so unwise as to leave yourself without faith in Jesus, you will not be able to stand against it. The Bible calls death "the king of terrors" (Job 18:13–14), and I have seen it terrorize grown men who have rejected God. It is fearsome to see, but much, much worse to experience.

So whatever you do in this precious life of yours, don't reject the Savior and die in your sins. God has made the way to be saved very simple. He says that each of us is in terrible danger, and He kindly provided a way for us to get what we don't deserve. That's called "mercy." We can avoid the just desert of Hell and instead have the undeserved gift of everlasting life. But whatever you do, don't get "religious." Don't try to clean up your life. You and I are like the thief on the cross. He couldn't go anywhere, he couldn't do anything. He was pinned to the cross by the unforgiving nails of Roman civil law. All he could do was turn to Jesus and say, "Lord, remember me . . ." (Luke 23:42).

In the same way, we can't do anything to save ourselves, because we are condemned by the merciless law of God. All we can do is turn to Jesus and say, "Lord, remember me." The moment you come to know Him as Lord and trust Him as Savior, you will forever banish any "what-ifs." Again, this is because faith comes as a gift from God. He will *give* you faith. He will help you in your unbelief by giving you a new heart and new desires. You will *want* to love, trust in, and obey everything God would have you do. And total trust doesn't allow any fear in the light of the knowledge of God. Fear is for unbelievers.

Always keep in mind that the most important moment of your life will be the instant of your death. Don't be like the man who neglected his eternal salvation. Jesus said that God said, "Fool. This night your soul will be required of you" (Luke 12:20). In other words, there's a debt that has to be paid. Hell required him. Death wanted its wages.

If you are considering these thoughts, please don't worry about what your unbelieving friends or family think. Worry about what *God* thinks. If they are your friends, they will respect you no matter what you believe. But if they turn on you like a pack of vicious hyenas, they were never your friends in the first place. You will have lost nothing.

Your life is without price, and you will lose it without the Savior. Seek Him with all of your heart. Jesus suffered and died on a cruel Cross so that God could extend mercy toward you. He rose from the dead so that you could live free from the fear of and the power of death. His gift to you is eternal life. Such is God's love for you. Do you believe that? For your sake I hope you do.

So make sure you choose the carpenter's cup. Choose to trust Jesus Christ. Confess and forsake your sins and willfully put your reliance (your trust) in Jesus right now, and you will come to know Him whom to know is life eternal. I can't express to you what a joy it is to me, what amazing consolation, what an absolute hope I have in Christ. Death has lost its sting completely. This is how Scripture explains it:

> Therefore we do not lose heart. Even though our outward man is perishing, yet the inward man is being renewed day by day. For our light affliction, which is but for a moment, is working for us a far more exceeding and eternal weight of glory, while we do not look at the things which are seen, but at the things which are not seen. For the things which are seen are temporary, but the things which are not seen are eternal (2 Corinthians 4:16–18).

You had no choice to be born. You just found yourself alive. You had no choice where you were to be born. You just found yourself in a certain country, speaking a certain language. You didn't choose your looks or your personality. But this day, God Himself will enable you to make a choice when it comes to your eternal destiny. He will give you repentance (see 2 Timothy 2:25). Will you seek God or won't you? Choose wisely. You have only one chance at life. Don't blow it.

> *Ray, was Thunderf00t[62] telling the truth in his "post-amble" when he relates, "The thing I really remember was that Ray believes in witches, wizards, demons, and sorcerers."*

If you don't believe that witches exist, simply Google the word "witches," and you will get 10.6 million results. If as an atheist you believe that seeing is believing, I'm sure one will accommodate you. So it's true that I believe that witches exist. Do I believe that these folks that are involved in witchcraft are capable of casting spells? I have no idea, but they try.

Do I believe in wizards? I sure do. I preached in "Speaker's Corner" in the city of Christchurch (population 350,000 — http://en.wikipedia.org/wiki/Christchurch) almost every day for 12 years, and crossed swords many times with "The Wizard of Christchurch." I took the first lunch hour and he took the second. "Jack" was a *very* good open-air speaker. He hated Christians, but often after he heckled me (he was easily my best heckler) we would go off together for a cup of tea. We also swapped birthday and Christmas presents. At times he would even let me get onto his ladder and preach the gospel to his crowd.

He was deeply into cosmology and graduated from the University of Leeds with a double honors degree in psychology and sociology. He practiced sorcery regularly, much to the delight of the general public. If you don't believe he existed because you don't believe in wizards, you can see some rare footage of my old friendly enemy on YouTube.[63]

I also believe in demons. This isn't only because the Bible says that they possess people and hold them in bondage to sin, but because I have had the eye-opening experience of casting them out of people a number of times (many years ago). You can read of these hair-raising experiences in the book *Out of the Comfort Zone*[64] in a chapter called "Hair Raisers." I wouldn't read it at night, if I were you.

> *I don't want to go to Hell . . . it sounds awful. However, to devote my entire life to avoiding such a fate I would need to have at least a little bit of credible evidence that Hell exists, which thus far I have yet to hear despite going to church weekly for 18 years and frequenting this blog for several months. Some say the evidence should be in my conscience, but I really do not feel any guilt when I lust after a woman or work on the Sabbath, so I will need more than just that. Any insight from Ray or any of the other Christians on this blog would be much appreciated.*

Start with John 3:12: "If I have told you earthly things and you do not believe, how will you believe if I tell you heavenly things?" God is always right on creation, history, kings, hearts, etc. So He is also right on the heavenly things.

Millions go to church and don't know the Lord. The Bible warns that in the last days there will be a "form of godliness." A "form" means that it's not genuine. It's just an outward appearance, and that certainly is what we see today. You managed to stick it out for 18 years. Many suffer the boredom of religion for a lifetime and tragically still die unsaved.

The way some deal with the thought of Hell is to pretend that God doesn't exist. But think for a moment of Stonehenge — the famous British formation of rocks. Why do people make such a song and dance about the assemblage of a few rocks? Because of its amazing formation. Its existence tells us that it was intelligently designed. No one in his right mind could think that it just happened by itself. It has composition. Yet the atheist looks at all the amazing structure in this beautifully balanced planet and says that there was no Designer. So atheism is ruled out for a "thinker."

The next refuge for a sin-loving sinner is the sin of "idolatry." That's when you concede that there is a God but you make one up in your own mind. A convenient "god" to have is one who has no sense of justice and therefore couldn't care less about whether or not the wicked are punished. Both atheism and idolatry allow guilt-free lust, pornography, fornication, adultery, and whatever else comes to our sinful minds. However, idolatry is delusional. Making up a nonexistent "god" is ridiculous. So it's ruled out for a thinker.

That leaves a Creator who is intelligent enough to have a sense of right and wrong. That leaves those who have sinned in big trouble, but we will only be aware of our sins if our God-given conscience is doing its duty. Do you know why leprosy is such a horrible disease? It's because it destroys one's sense of pain. Instead of moving his body around when sitting or sleeping because of mild pain, a leper remains still, and that stops the blood flow, causing the flesh to rot. When your conscience no longer causes you pain, it will let your very soul rot with the disease of sin.

Have you ever watched a movie where you are longing for the evil guy to get what's coming to him? When he gets it, you rejoice. It's a good feeling when justice is done. Guess what? We *are* the evil guy. The best of us are filled with lying, stealing, lust, greed, envy, ingratitude, self-righteousness, blasphemy — blinded by our love for sin. And when all that sin comes out on the Day of Judgment, Hell will be what we have justly coming to us. Justice will be done. God offers you mercy in the Savior He provided. Ignore Him at your own eternal peril.

So if I were to blaspheme the Holy Spirit would you still try to convert me?

I can't "convert" a soul. It's *God* that does the converting. However, I will continue to plead with you and others to seek His mercy as long as I have a heartbeat.

There was a group of folks who received national publicity some time ago who aired videos of themselves online, saying that they were blaspheming God. They were called "The Blasphemy Challenge," and their challenge was, "Do you dare accept the Blasphemy Challenge? Show the world how sure you are that the Christian God doesn't exist!"

I knew (and liked) their leader, so I e-mailed him with a little advice. I reminded him that the name "God," when translated into Arabic, is "Allah," and that it wasn't wise in today's political climate to create a video of yourself saying (when translated into Arabic), "My name is such and such, and I blaspheme Allah, and I am not afraid." Moslems have murdered those who have mocked their prophet (let alone their god), and they threatened a school teacher with death simply because she named a teddy bear after him.

Since sending that e-mail I have noticed that the leader of "The Blasphemy Challenge" seems to have disappeared. My friend Brian Sapient used a fake name, but the faces and real names of those atheists who responded to his challenge are still permanently on the Internet for all the world to see. If I was one of them, I would be praying.

Ray — what will you do to pass the time when you get to Heaven? Your ministry is obviously a great passion and a great motivating factor. What will you do to pass the time for eternity with no one to save?

Think for a moment of the best meal around which you have wrapped your salivating lips. Think of the most amazing animals and fish you have ever seen, or the most breath-taking snow-capped mountains, or tall green trees. Think of the greatest moment of pleasure you have experienced, whether it was an intimate moment (I may as well say that because it will no doubt come to mind) or whether it was seeing the birth of your first child. Think of pictures you have seen of amazing blue waters lapping onto the white sands of a beautiful beach.

Then pull all those amazingly pleasurable thoughts into one vision of joy and drop them in a trash bin where they belong. This is because this entire creation is under the Curse of Almighty God. He gave us all those pleasures (including sex), but they are absolutely nothing compared to what He has in store for those who love Him (see 1 Corinthians 2:9).

The Bible says God subjected all things to "futility." Every pleasure is part of this "fallen" and cursed creation and is fleeting. It doesn't last. It's momentary. And then it becomes a memory, and in time death will come to you and take you into eternity.

This is the message of the entire Book of Ecclesiastes. King Solomon made the wealth of Bill Gates look like pocket change and the wisdom of our most intelligent contemporary sound like the mumblings of a dummy. He was super wise and filthy rich, and yet he lamented, "All is vanity and grasping for the wind." It was nothing but chasing the wind, because of the reality of impending death.

So, what will I do for eternity? I will enjoy "pleasures forevermore." I will get to inherit this earth, but it will be changed — remodeled, transformed, new, and utterly improved. The Genesis Curse will be removed. That means no pain, no tears, no disease, no suffering, no death, and no futility. Not an ounce.

I will no longer desperately seek to save those who are heading for Hell. Then it will be too late. The door of God's mercy will be closed. He says that if you want filth, you will have it and what it entails for eternity. But for all who repent and trust the Savior, even our memories will be reconditioned. We won't remember "the former things."

So what are you going to be doing for eternity? Please join us. See www.needGod.com for details of what to do.

I see no reason to become a Christian. None at all.

I had a dream. I was riding my bike around a corner when I saw three hungry-looking jaguars waiting for me. They were massively powerful, and the first one's eyes had a look of absolute determination. I didn't take the time to look into the eyes of the other two.

I knew I couldn't outpace them, but I desperately tried. It was no use. In seconds I would be dead meat. Do you know what I did to get away from them? I woke up.

You have a terrifying three-fold dilemma in front of you. Death is waiting around the corner. Every day you look into its cold eyes. You can't outpace it. It will only be a matter of time until you are dead meat.

After death, something worse awaits you. It is eternal justice. It has absolute and resolute determination that you get what is coming to you. Once sealed in eternity, you cannot escape divine equity.

But there is one more terror in this nightmare in which you find yourself. If you die in your sins, a place of punishment in Hell waits for you. There, perfect justice will be done.

Do you know what you have to do to get out of this nightmare? Simply wake up. Stop dreaming about the brainless and unscientific mythology of evolution. It is a dead-end path. It's based on an unfounded faith, not on proof. Stop the insane and rebellious dream that God doesn't exist and that there will be no ultimate retribution. It's coming. God will punish lust as adultery, hatred of one's brother as murder, and all liars, thieves, and fornicators. You will even have to give an account of every idle word that you have spoken.

You have His offer of mercy through the blood of the Cross — the Savior suffered for your sins, then defeated death on the third day. The escape is there. You need not be a slave to death.

Salvation in Jesus is universal (see Isaiah 55:1–7). If you repent and trust the Savior, it doesn't matter who you are or what background you come from — darker colored skin to lighter colored skin, Jews and Gentiles, Protestants and Catholics, will be able to join hands and sing in the words of the old Negro spiritual, "Free at last! Free at last! Thank God Almighty, we are free at last!"

There probably isn't a God. I'd never be stupid enough to commit myself 100 percent to the statement that "THERE DEFINITELY IS NO GOD!" because I don't know it for a fact. It's summer here in the UK, so I can look out my window and say, for a fact, "The sky definitely is blue." You could say that to a color-blind person the sky isn't blue, but you'd be wrong because the color-blind person has a vision deficiency causing them to see incorrectly.

I appreciate the fact that you have illustrated my point. As an agnostic, you can't be sure of anything in this life. You can't be sure if God exists. You can't be sure of evolution. You can't be sure of what is right and what is wrong. But you are sure that the sky is blue. However, it's not. It has no color at all. You see blue because sunlight is scattered by oxygen and nitrogen in the atmosphere. So it appears blue to you, but it really isn't blue. The only thing you can be sure of is your death.

On the other hand, those who know God (as opposed to those who simply "believe" in His existence) can be sure of many things. This is because God is never wrong. Ever. He is absolutely trustworthy in that which He says. We can therefore know absolutely about our origins, and we can know absolutely what is right and what is wrong. There is no "probably" when it comes to His immutable promises.

Rather than let this fact upset you, see it instead as unspeakably good news for those who are tossed back and forth on the sea of speculation. It means that you can have a solid foundation for this life and absolute hope (know that you have everlasting life) in the next.

I was just wondering, Ray, why did you move to the U. S. — why come to America since it is so Christian? Why not go to a country that is primarily Hindu or Buddhist or atheistic? According to polls, about 85 percent of Americans consider themselves Christians and at least 35–40 percent call themselves "born again" while only 10–12 percent of Americans are atheists. . . . Aside from this blog aren't you pretty much preaching to the choir in the U.S.?

I was honored to be invited to come to this country back in 1989. I had been speaking in Hawaii in 1988 when the pastor of a church in California heard what I was saying, called me in New Zealand some time later, and said, "America must hear this message!" So at his church's kind invitation and clear direction from God, I uprooted my family and came to the United States.

I already knew that He was going to bring me here (see *Out of the Comfort Zone* for details) and I knew why. I had discovered the reason that this nation in particular was filled with so many "false converts." A false convert is a person who says that he is a Christian, but his life doesn't match what he professes to believe. Some stay within the Church as false converts, but many are exposed by "tribulation, temptation, and persecution" and go back to the sinful world (as the Bible says) like a dog returns to its vomit (see 2 Peter 2:22). Your own experience is an example of a false conversion:

> I was brought up in a Christian home and accepted Christ as my savior at the age of 14. I committed my life to full-time Christian service at 18. I am a graduate of a conservative Christian college and seminary, having studied the Bible formally at the college level for six years and as a Christian for many more years than that. I was in Christian ministry for over 20 years. So I guess you could at least say I am very familiar with the Bible and its teachings. I don't know if it would surprise you or not, but I know several other preachers who have rejected the tenets of Christianity after having been in the ministry for many years.

You stayed in the Church for many years and were able to fake it even longer than the well-known false convert and former pastor, Mr. Dan Barker.[65] But nowhere in the Bible does it say to "accept" Christ as your Savior. That was the root cause of your problem.

My problem is that people who have had a false conversion are often bitter and angry (as with Mr. Barker) and therefore unreachable with the true gospel. I hope that's not your case. If you are interested in the details of why you fell away, please take the time to listen to "Hell's Best Kept Secret" and then "True and False Conversion" on livingwaters.com (there's no charge).

The stories [my grandmother] tells are quite vivid. If I didn't know better, I'd believe every word she said. I, and other family members, sometimes feel the need to bring her back to reality, but most of the time, we realize that it's futile to try. I'm not suggesting that your mental condition is comparable to a 72-year-old woman with Alzheimer's (I would never insult my grandmother like that), but when you, or anyone else, claims to "know God," I can only assume that you're in a state of hallucination.

What's the basis for your assumption that you are the one who is sane and that your grandmother is not? Here are a few test questions: Do you believe that there is a creation without a Creator? Do you believe a woman has the right to kill her child in the womb? Should homosexuals have the right to marry each other? What is the purpose of your existence (other than to find happiness while you are here)? What is your definition of a sane person? How do you know your definition is the correct one? Does your grandmother think that she is a primate? Do you think she is? Do you believe Richard Dawkins is correct when he says that we are all primates? If there is one chance in a million that God exists, and He is offering you everlasting life, would you take the time to look into it?

God says we can know Him. So either God is the authority about matters of God or *you*, a human, are claiming to be the ultimate authority — in other words, you are claiming to be God. This is the religion of humanism. It is better to leave God as the authority on matters relating to God (Psalm 118:8; NIV).

Can a truly saved Christian believe in evolution? If not then does that mean we need to believe in a literal flood, young earth creation perspective, etc.?

A Christian can believe in fairies, if he wishes. While I wouldn't doubt the salvation of one who did, I may doubt his sanity. This is because Christianity doesn't come from "what you believe" (although that is part of the equation), it comes from who you know. Let me back up a little to explain what I mean. The Bible teaches that Jesus Christ was pre-existent before He was manifest in human form. He claimed to be the source of life, saying things like "I am the life" (see John 1:4, 11:25, 14:6). When someone repents and believes the gospel (that Jesus Christ died for his sin and rose on the third day), he places his trust in the Savior and comes to "know" God. Then God "seals" the believer with the Holy Spirit. Jesus Christ "who is our life" dwells within the believer (see John 14:16–18). The Scriptures say "Christ, who is in you" (see Colossians 1:27). Jesus said that He would come to and would actually dwell within the Christian through the Holy Spirit (see John 14:21).

Here now is the bottom line. If you have Jesus Christ, you have life, regardless of your denomination. God knows those who love Him. If you don't have Jesus Christ (through the new birth of John 3:3), you don't have life. You are still dead in your sins and justly under the condemnation of God (see John 3:17–18). Here are the pivotal verses:

> He who has the Son has life; he who does not have the Son of God does not have life. These things I have written to you who believe in the name of the Son of God, that you may know that you have eternal life (1 John 5:12–13).

That said, if you have the Son of God, then the Holy Spirit will lead you into all truth (see John 16:13). Your theology in time will become "sound," and you will align your beliefs with those truths revealed in Holy Scripture, because it is God's revelation to mankind. If the Old Testament says there was a literal Flood (Jesus did also), the Christian cannot believe otherwise. If the Bible says that the earth freely floats in space when "science" of the time said that it didn't (see Job 26:7), the Christian quickly sides with the Bible. If they don't, they are inconsistent, but that doesn't mean they can't be saved.

In the case of evolution, Scripture is very clear that God made man in His image (not as a primate). He made him and all the animal kingdom as male and female, and He gave them (and every living animal) the ability to procreate "after their own kind," and not to evolve in time into other "kinds" of animals. We see the truth of all of the above in both the fossil record and the creation that surrounds us. ("Evolutionary biology is unable to reveal why animals would abandon asexual reproduction in favor of more costly and inefficient sexual reproduction."[66])

God knows that I will have eggs for breakfast tomorrow. I don't — I haven't made up my mind yet. But when I wake up in the morning and select eggs for breakfast, was it ever possible for me to choose otherwise? Either I cannot choose toast instead of eggs, or God was incorrect when He saw that I would pick eggs. And we all know that God is never wrong. . . . So where is my free will?

Either God exists or He doesn't. To say that there is no Creator means that everything happened by chance, from nothing. To say that there was no initial cause means that I think it was causeless. If on the other hand I say that an intelligent Creator brought creation into existence, then I can't limit Him, because the creation itself is a revelation of His unlimited supernatural ability.

If you think otherwise, try making an eye yourself, from nothing. Do you start with the 137 million light sensitive cells, or the nerve endings, or the retina? How do you make a retina from nothing? We have no idea where or how to begin. The Bible asks the question, "He who formed the eye, shall he not see?" In other words, if God has the genius (for want of a better word) to create the eye, reason tells us that He's not blind.

If He can create the brain of a man, He can therefore see the thoughts of a man. The eye of the Lord is in every place, beholding the evil and the good. Nothing is hidden from the eyes of Him with whom we have to give an account. When the Bible speaks of nothing, it means "nothing." Nothing is hidden from God. That means He sees your thought life, every hair on your head, every atom He created, and every event in the future of time.

Now, to your toast and eggs. The fact that God sees the future has nothing to do with your choice of breakfast. He doesn't choose your menu. You do. He simply knows the path you will take. If you find that hard to reconcile, think of it like this. If you see a live sporting event and then go home and watch the same game on TV, you may know the outcome but you don't determine the result.

An atheist questioned my relationship with God, the reality of which I likened to my relationship with my wife. Jay wrote: "I'll first note that the description of knowing the Lord given here is different from any marriage I've ever seen, and certainly nothing like mine. I interact with my wife; I talk to her verbally and hear her audibly. I embrace her to show my love, and she embraces back. Sometimes we have differing opinions that lead to arguments. We often take walks in the evening with our dog, and discuss the day's events. I try to comfort her when she's upset, and she does the same for me. I do trust her implicitly and she is always in my thoughts." I wrote back, "I don't believe your wife exists. Prove she does. Until then, I think that she is a figment of your imagination."

He said, "I've sent an e-mail to the address you usually ask that correspondences be sent. It contains a picture of me and wife, taken outside the MGM Casino in Las Vegas last month."

"How do I know that's your wife?"

"I will also take a photo of my marriage license if you wish (with certain information redacted of course)."

"I think it's one of those bogus five-dollar Vegas marriage licenses or something you have done on Photoshop."

"I'll have to require you to make an effort to come meet her. We live in the upstate of South Carolina. You as well as your family are more than welcome to come spend some time with us if you are ever in the area. We'll gladly take you out to dinner at our expense."

"Thank you for your kind hospitality, but you could easily find an actress who could pretend to be your wife."

"I've provided you with as much evidence as is available to me at this moment, and I'm perfectly willing to provide more upon request."

"You have provided me with no evidence at all. I do not believe the woman you say is your wife exists. Therefore, in my mind, she doesn't exist.

"The truth is, you can't prove to me that she is your wife if I have the presupposition that she doesn't exist, and I'm not open to 'reason.'

"Creation is 100 percent proof that there is a Creator *to anyone open to reason*. For some reason, I am surrounded on this blog by unreasonable people — those who aren't open to reason. But I will keep trying to reach you (and others) as long as I have life in me.

"Thanks for writing. Love to your wife."

A few night[s] back I had a dream about the rapture. In this dream I was lifted off the ground. Floating in the air, I suddenly realized I was wrong and there is a God and I'm in a lot of trouble. Then everyone around me, and me, stopped, hung in the air, then fell to the ground; but we didn't hit the ground, we went straight through it. Down we went into Hell. I didn't think to pray or call out to Jesus. I just thought to myself "This is impossible, this can't be happening . . . hang on, this is just a dream!" And that was the end of that. The thing is, Ray, as realistic as the dream was, it didn't make me want to repent at all.

Most parents have had dreams of one of their kids being in great danger, or we have nightmares about horrible spiders, or falling from the edge of a cliff. I have had a recurring dream for years in which I was in a pulpit in front of a huge crowd and I couldn't find my place in the Bible. We tend to dream our fears, but that one fear resulted in a positive outcome. I always step up to a pulpit knowing exactly where I am going, and that happens because of that horrible dream.

You mentioned that the dream you had didn't cause you to want to repent. That's understandable. Many people "repent" out of fear and end up falling away. The problem is, repentance must be coupled with what the Bible calls "godly sorrow." There must be contrition.

Think of a man who has committed adultery, who wants to get back with his wife. She is willing to take him back, but what is she looking for? Genuine sorrow that will result in him not wanting to betray her trust ever again.

That's what God is looking for in you — a genuine sorrow that will result in you turning from all that you know to be offensive to Him.

It sounds a little ridiculous when an adult "dares" someone to do something. But I will be ridiculous in a big way to make an important point. I *double*-dare you to say to God, "Please show me as You see me, and then show me Yourself, as You are." Before you do this, read through the Sermon on the Mount (Matthew 5–7).

Wait a second . . . I think I've figured out the ruse here. At some point, Ray is going to blog about a comment from this post and say that in order to "believe" in extraterrestrial life, we'd have to have knowledge of the entire universe. Then we'll be told that if we "believe" in extraterrestrial life, we should have no trouble believing in his God. Does that about sum it up, Ray? Did I pick your petty ploy?

Unfortunately, you are incorrect in your assessments on two counts. The first mistake you have made is to think that you have to have absolute knowledge to believe in something. Rather, you have to have absolute knowledge to say that you know that something doesn't exist. You and I can believe in anything we want. Our belief makes no difference to reality. Truth is, despite our beliefs.

But God, who is omniscient, made no comment about creating life elsewhere in the universe. It is Heaven in many places, but that would be the third Heaven(i.e., presence of God). Furthermore, there would be theological problems if they did exist: (1) they would be cursed due to sin (Romans 8:22), and (2) they would have no possibility of salvation, by not being a descendant of Adam. Jesus became a man to die for man once and for all (Hebrews 7:24).

The second incorrect assessment (which is built on the first) is the thought that if we believe in aliens, we should have no trouble believing in God. But there's a huge difference between believing in aliens and believing in God. There is no evidence that aliens exist. Scientists can only suppose that there is a possibility that they exist, somewhere.

However, every single "made" thing in this creation is absolute 100 percent evidence that God exists. You cannot have things that are made without having a Maker. It's a scientific impossibility. You cannot have a creation without a Creator. Nothing material can exist without a beginning — "In the beginning God created the heavens and the earth" (Genesis 1:1). "All things were made through Him, and without Him nothing was made that was made" (John 1:3).

²² By faith ᶠJoseph, when he was dying, made mention of the departure of the children of Israel, and gave instructions concerning his bones.

The Faith of Moses

²³ By faith ᵍMoses, when he was born, was hidden three months by his parents, because they saw he was a beautiful child; and they were not afraid of the ʰking's command.

²⁴ By faith ᶦᵢ...

Chapter Five

Religion: God and Atheism

If God exists, why didn't He kill Hitler before he killed six million Jews?

Hitler was guilty of causing more than six million deaths. If those people had not been murdered, many of them would have had children of their own. Hitler not only killed them, but in a sense he also killed their offspring. However, he didn't commit those atrocities alone. He employed men such as Heinrich Himmler who willingly carried out his plan of mass murder. So it would make sense that if God were to have stopped Hitler by killing him, he should also have killed each one of those evil men because they were also potential mass murderers.

You may not be aware that Stalin was guilty of what was called "forced famine." His starvation plan resulted in the cruel and slow deaths of seven million men, women, and children. God should have killed him also. He should have also killed those responsible for the genocide of Bosnia-Herzegovina. Between 1992 and 1995, more than 200,000 men, women, and children lost their lives.

Then there were those who ran around with machetes slashing people to death in Rwanda in 1994. That resulted in the horrific deaths of 800,000 men, women, and children.

Don't forget Pol Pot and all those smashed-in skulls in Cambodia. Between 1975 and 1979, his regime took two million lives.

Add to that the "rape of Nanking" between 1937 and 1938 in China by Japanese troops that caused 300,000 deaths, and the murders of 1.5 million Armenians in Turkey between 1915 and 1918.

They were the *mass* murderers of the 20th century that God would have had the right to kill before they carried out their plans.

Now here is an important question. Should God have also killed Jeffrey Dahmer before he killed and ate 18 young men? Of course. It is estimated that Ted Bundy murdered more than 100 people, and John Wayne Gacy killed 33. They should be included in the God-should-have-killed-them list.

How about those who committed mass killings in the workplace and schools in recent years? Then there were those wicked murderers who took the lives of 200,000 people during the 1990s. That's how many people were murdered *just in the United States* in that one ten-year period. Worldwide deaths by murder is much higher than 200,000. They *have* to be added to the list, if we want God to do the "right" thing.

How about drunken drivers who slaughter innocent people on our roads? Should He kill them before they get behind the wheel? Yep. That makes sense. Suicide bombers? Of course. What about those who have killed thousands by putting bombs on planes and trains? How about the murderous Mafia bosses? Then there are those who kidnap, torture, and rape people.

If God started killing off people before they did evil, there would be a lot of people being struck by lightning (or by whatever means God chose to kill them). In fact, it would be all of us. However, there is some good news for those who would like to see the guilty get what they deserve. God *has* set aside a Day in which He will judge the world in righteousness. There will be a resurrection of all people, and on that day Hitler will get exactly what's coming to him.

But then again, if God is perfect and holy, and He sees lust as adultery and hatred as murder, that leaves us *all* in big trouble. That's where the Cross comes in. Those who repent and trust the Savior receive forgiveness of sins and the gift of everlasting life.

You may not be a mass murderer, but your sins are extremely serious in the sight of a holy God. So make sure you don't end up in Hell with Hitler. You can be sure that he will receive "greater condemnation," but that will be no consolation for you if you also find yourself in Hell.

There are a number of times in Scripture where God instantly judged men and women for their sins. He killed a couple of men (in the Old Testament) because of their sexual sins. Others were judged for homosexuality and idolatry. A couple dropped dead simply for lying. Imagine if God treated you according to your sins right now! But He hasn't, because He's "rich in mercy."

At this moment in time you have before you judgment or mercy, life or death, Heaven or Hell. So forget about Hitler and take some time to think seriously about your own sins. Think about your "secret" sins that God sees, and then think about the Savior and what He did for rebellious sinners such as us.

Religion has no relevance in contemporary America. We are a secular nation. We don't need God.

There was a time in the United States when public schools opened in prayer every day. These were the words kids recited along with the Pledge of Allegiance: "Almighty God, we acknowledge our dependence upon Thee, and we beg Thy blessings upon us, our parents, our teachers, and our country." I believe that the liberty to pray and read the Bible in schools was given by God as an unalienable right:

> ". . . All men are created equal, that they are endowed by their Creator with certain unalienable Rights [a right that is 'not to be taken away'], that among these are Life, Liberty and the pursuit of Happiness." Declaration of Independence, July 4, 1776

However, after one atheist complained that it was unconstitutional for her son to pray in school, in 1963 the Supreme Court ruled eight to one in favor of abolishing school prayer and Bible reading in the public schools.

They did this by creating something called "a wall of separation between church and state" (a phrase not found in the Constitution). However, up until that time the only "wall" was the wall that was put there by the framers of the Bill of Rights (ten amendments to the Constitution) to keep the government from stripping America of its God-given liberties:

> *Congress shall make no law respecting an establishment of religion, or prohibiting the free exercise thereof;* or abridging the freedom of speech, or of the press; or the right of the people peaceably to assemble, and to petition the government for a redress of grievances [emphasis added].[67]

Essentially, the court case switched the United States from Christian-based to atheistic-based. The U.S. Supreme Court now forces atheism as the state religion. Tragically, in 1995 Madalyn Murray O'Hair, the atheist who had prayer banned in schools, was murdered by another atheist. Police found her body in 2001. It had been cut up with a saw. In 1980 her son was baptized as a Christian and went on to become a Baptist preacher.

Regardless of whether you believe Jesus or you believe Ray, people who had never heard the gospel are burning in Hell [and] that makes your God evil.

> . . . the LORD searches all hearts and understands all the intent of the thoughts. If you seek Him, He will be found by you; but if you forsake Him, He will cast you off forever (1 Chronicles 28:9).

> Seek the LORD your God, and you will find Him if you seek Him with all your heart and with all your soul (Deuteronomy 4:29).

You are presuming that people go to Hell because they have never heard the gospel, and then, upon that erroneous presumption, say, "Therefore God is unjust." However, people go to Hell for murder, rape, adultery, lying, stealing, hatred, evil imaginations, blasphemy, etc. God owes no one mercy. All He owes us is justice. Equity is His moral obligation.

Like most atheists, you have a wrong understanding of the nature of God. This is because atheists create a god who has no sense of right or wrong, justice or truth. Their god is an unloving and merciless tyrant. But (as I have said many times) the concept of the god they don't believe in doesn't exist. He is a figment of their imagination (the place of imagery). The creation of a false god is called "idolatry," and it's a violation of the first and the second of the Ten Commandments.

There is a short-term payoff with idolatry. Not only can you spit out blasphemy against God and feel justified, but it also gives you a temporary license to sin your heart out without any fear of having to answer to Him for your actions. Idolatry opens wide the door to the joys of pornography, fornication, lust, adultery, and any other darling sin you wish to name. There is short-term pleasure but eternal consequences. However, that is your choice. It's not mine, and because I care about you I will do all I can to warn you that you will eternally regret your decision.

Look at what the Bible says about Moses and the joys of sin:

> By faith Moses, when he became of age, refused to be called the son of Pharaoh's daughter, choosing rather to suffer affliction with the people of God than to enjoy the passing pleasures of sin, esteeming the reproach of Christ greater riches than the treasures in Egypt; for he looked to the reward (Hebrews 11:24–26).

You have that same choice. You can enjoy the pleasures of sin for a season, or you can repent, trust the Savior, and find everlasting life.

Repent of your sins and accept Jesus! As long as you do it before you die you should be fine, so have fun while you're young, and become saved later in life. It's a bit of a gamble, but then again, so is choosing from the thousands of religions that say they are right. Christianity, the religion that allows you to live your life however you want and get saved right before dying, it's awesome!

These are the words of someone who is deluded into thinking that God is a fool. He thinks that he will play the ultimate bait and switch. However, deathbed conversions are few and far between. More than 40,000 people are killed each year in car accidents. I wonder how many thought that they would have an opportunity to give God their leftovers but didn't, and instead will be justly damned for their sins. Those who think that they can fool God should read the last verses of Matthew 23 and see the fate of all who suffer from the same delusion.

My guess (from the language you use) is that you have been duped by those who think that becoming a Christian is a matter of "accepting Jesus." Neither does salvation come from "asking Jesus into your heart." You won't find either of those two popular phrases in the Bible. Salvation comes through repentance and trust in Jesus alone. No other way.

Keep in mind that in the next 24 hours, 150,000 people (many of whom were planning for a future on earth) are going to pass into eternity. Today may be the day God loses patience with you (see Luke 12:20). Please, make sure it doesn't come to that.

If I become a Christian, I will have to give up sex!

A little boy crept into his father's bedroom one night, grabbed his wallet, and stole a crisp new $20 bill. The next day his dad found out that he had stolen the money. He took him aside and said that he had especially saved that bill as a gift for the boy and was planning on giving it to him the next morning. The boy not only missed out on the gift, but he was punished for his theft.

It may come as a shock to the average atheist, but sex didn't evolve. It wasn't an accident. Male and female were created by God and given the ability to procreate. Its pleasure is a gift from God to each one of us. But we have taken the gift and perverted it through lust, fornication, and adultery. This may not be a concern at the moment, but it will be on Judgment Day. God sees lust as adultery and warns that fornicators will not enter Heaven.

God had lavished His goodness upon King David, but despite this, David's sinful heart still caused him to lust after another man's wife. He took her to himself and committed adultery, then he tried to cover his tracks when she became pregnant by murdering her husband. Yet God had mercy on him and upon his repentance and faith, forgave him. You can read the whole sordid story in 2 Samuel 11–12, and then David's penitent prayer in Psalm 51. It was written for our instruction (see 2 Timothy 3:16).

Is there free will in Heaven? If there is free will in Heaven is it possible to sin in Heaven? If the answer to either of those questions is no then clearly either free will is not as important as you make out OR it is possible for God to give people free will AND remove the ability for them to sin. God can apparently do anything. So why could he not have created beings that had both free will and lacked the ability to sin?

Most Christians believe that God allowed the Fall because He didn't want to make us as "robots." He therefore gave us a free will, and that entailed the freedom to choose right and wrong. That explanation has never satisfied me. This is because it is (hopefully) evident that in Heaven God isn't going to give the vast sea of redeemed humanity the ability to sin. That didn't work with just one couple, so it's not going to work with innumerable multitudes. So we will clearly live in a state where we aren't robots but we won't have the capability to sin. That makes sense.

The question then arises as to why God didn't do that with Adam and Eve. Why did He create them with the freedom of choice, and therefore allow them to bring all this misery, death, and an impending Hell upon the entire human race?

This sounds like it is more an issue of why permit sin. If God didn't give men rule over the earth, then how could they have been made in the image of a ruling God? But they *were*; so when they sinned, God permitted it because He gave them the ruling authority on earth. Had He stopped them from sinning, then they wouldn't have really had dominion, and God would have been deceiving them. Instead, God permitted it.

That's the first of two questions that I will humbly and with due reverence ask when I get to Heaven.

The second is, "Why does God allow children to suffer?" I'm not talking about suffering the pain of a broken leg or some sort of temporal disease. I'm talking about excruciating pain from a disease that sucks out their life, leaving them as a skeleton, and then takes them terrified to an untimely grave. If He is loving and kind, why doesn't He heal them? He has the power to do so. Nothing is impossible for God. So why not heal them? The atheist therefore concludes that God is either a tyrant or He doesn't exist.

Here's why I am still a Christian despite my unanswered questions. I know that the sun exists. I also know that it is directly responsible for the agonizing deaths of many innocent people. Deserts are littered with the dry bones of those who found themselves under its terrible burning heat. I know that there are holes in this analogy because the sun isn't a thinking, rational part of God's creation, but my point is, do I then conclude that the sun doesn't exist because it killed these people?

We are in a sin-cursed world. We are all sinners. We *all* sinned in *Adam* and we all deserve this and more. The fascinating thing is that not everyone goes through this, due to God's grace.

Consider Lamentations 5:7: "Our fathers sinned and are no more, but we bear their iniquities." Why make someone perfect in an imperfect world? Why not make them perfect in a perfect world? This is what God promised to do.

Consider also the horrible things people go through in light of 1 Corinthians 10:13. These people — including children — bear so much that it gives an idea how strong God made them.

I can't deny the reality of the existence of God simply because I have unanswered questions. I know He exists because of the axiom of creation. I know He exists because I know Him experientially and have an all-consuming love for Him that embraces all of my heart, mind, soul, and strength. I'm not angered, worried, frustrated, concerned, or upset by these questions, because I love and trust Him. I know that the time will come when I find out the answers, and I don't mind waiting.

How do you know God is of the Christian variety? Equally devout Muslims disagree. If I'm on the fence, I need a better answer than "I just KNOW. God has revealed himself to me."

Good question. The thing that makes Christianity utterly unique is the Cross. For it to make sense you have to back up from Jesus to Moses. He was the one who received the Ten Commandments from the hand of God. The law of Moses was given to reveal God's standard of "righteousness."

1. Christianity is based on grace, not works like other religions.
2. Big picture theology: The punishment from an infinite Creator God is an infinite punishment that must be satisfied. Good works do not offset this punishment — it must be paid for. Only Christ, who is God, can take the infinite punishment we all deserve. Only His death and Resurrection can cover our sin.

3. Unlike all other religious leaders, *only* Christ came back from the dead, proving He has power over death and proving that what He says happens after death is true.
4. Other religions must borrow from the Bible for absolute morality.

Now zoom forward about 1,500 years to the time of Jesus. He was God in human form who came to earth to "exalt the law and make it honorable" (Isaiah 42:21). You can see Him do that in the famous Sermon on the Mount (Matthew 5–7). During that sermon He quotes the Seventh Commandment (about adultery) and then says, "But I say to you that whoever looks at a woman to lust for her has already committed adultery with her in his heart" (Matthew 5:28). So let's think about that one commandment for a moment. If God is going to judge us on Judgment Day by that (very high) standard, who of us would be guiltless and avoid Hell?

So humanity has a problem. All of us have violated God's law since Adam and Eve. He is a perfect Judge, and we are guilty criminals, heading for a just and terrible punishment for our multitude of crimes against His law. So my prayers, my fasting, my helping others in that context aren't "good" works. If we offer the Judge anything as "payment" for our crimes, the Bible says it's an abomination to Him, because it is a detestable attempt to bribe Him, and He will not be bribed. Not for a millisecond. So the religion of "doing" things to merit God's favor is fruitless, in the truest sense of the word.

So how can we be saved from His wrath? Only by the mercy of the Judge. God Himself became a person in Jesus Christ, suffered on a cruel Cross, and then rose again on the third day. That Cross was the complete payment for our crimes against God and His law. We broke the law of Moses, but Jesus paid our fine. That means that the Judge can (upon our repentance and faith in Jesus) completely dismiss our case. Everlasting life is the free gift of God (see Ephesians

2:8–9). It can't be earned by "religious" works, and therein is the uniqueness of Christianity. Take it or leave it, but do so at your own eternal peril. See John 8:31–32 and John 14:21 for more details.

> Though He was a Son, yet He learned obedience by the things which He suffered. And having been perfected, He became the author of eternal salvation to all who obey Him (Hebrews 5:8–9).

An atheist said, "So what should we believe instead . . . (God) just 'poofed' everything into existence?"

A Christian named Carl responded: What about the "poofs" *you* have faith in?

Poof! Explosive dust cloud to planetary systems and galaxies!

Poof! Bacteria from primordial soup!

Poof! Cambrian explosion!

Poof! Invertebrates to vertebrates!

Poof! Fish to land animals!

Poof! Dinosaurs to birds!

Poof! Reptiles to mammals!

Poof! Apes to man!

Lots of poof but no proof. John 1:3 says, "All things were made through Him, and without Him nothing was made that was made." I suggest going back to the beginning in Genesis and letting God tell you what He did. Because this is the issue . . . either God is the authority or man is. So who are you going to place your absolute authority in: a perfect, all-knowing God who has always been there or fallible, sinful human beings who weren't there?

> *I became an atheist to distance myself from people like you, but since becoming an atheist I've found that I don't care — I honestly don't care — if there is a God. I don't care if there is an afterlife. I don't care if I'm going to Hell. Oh, you can say all you want about that, I just don't care. You can't save me.*

And I don't believe a word you are saying. If you became an atheist to distance yourself from people like me, why are you writing to me? You may say that you don't care, but you do, and so do I.

I care enough to get up on a soapbox thousands of times and look like a fool, to plead with people like you who either say that they don't care about their eternal welfare, or show that they don't by their godless lifestyle.

But the Bible teaches that sinful mankind doesn't "care" about God. He gave them life itself and they don't care. He gave them eyes to see His incredible creation, ears to listen to incredible music, taste buds to enjoy incredible food, and they don't care. As the Psalmist says, "God is in none of his thoughts" (Psalm 10:4), and yet at the same time they vainly use His name as a cuss word.

If you had to give up one of those senses, which would it be? Sight? You don't care if you go blind? How about giving up your taste? Or your hearing? Imagine never seeing a beautiful rose or a sunset or the color blue ever again, or never tasting good food or hearing the music of a bird in the early morning. If you are sane, you care.

But the loss of those precious senses is nothing compared to giving up your soul. You "soul" is the real you. It's the interchangeable Bible word for your life. Your soul looks out the windows you call "eyes." It's your soul that responds to the 10,000 friendly little taste buddies on your tongue. Your soul listens to the amazing sounds that are pulled into your inner ear. You don't know what you have until it's gone. Familiarity does breed contempt. Jesus said that if a man gained the entire world but lost his soul, he is the biggest of losers.

Yet every day more than 80 Americans "don't care" enough to take their own lives. Life's circumstances have tragically driven them to that terrible point. Atheism is your first step in that direction. You owe it nothing.

You are right about one thing, though. I can't save you. Only God can. So after you have read these words of mine, how about reading the words of God? Read Matthew chapters 5–7 and get a glimpse of His perfect holiness. Then think about how we all justly deserve Hell if God is that holy, and think about how Jesus cared enough to take your punishment upon Himself — to pay your fine so that the Judge of the universe could dismiss your case. What more could you want?

Do you ever doubt the existence of God? And if so, why?

Do I ever doubt the existence of God? Not for a moment. However, an intellectual belief in God's existence is really a nonissue. This is why: I live in a solid, well-made house. Do I ever doubt the existence of a builder? Not for a moment. My wife has a well-made and reliable vehicle. Do I ever doubt (for some strange reason) the existence of a car maker? Not for a moment. I own a well-made computer . . . I'm sure you get the message. I never doubt that there was a maker of these things, because these things can't make themselves. Romans 1 tells me that they *had* to be made by someone with an intelligent mind. The alternative is ludicrous.

The issue I think you may be driving at is rather, "Does my faith in God ever waver?" The answer to that one is the same. Do I ever doubt God? Not for a moment. There's a reason for this unwavering faith. If you asked me if I ever waver when it comes to faith in my wife, I would answer the same — not for a moment. This is because I trust her with all of my heart. She is a trustworthy person. She *always* keeps her word. However, there is a possibility that she could let me down. That could happen because she is a sinner. She is fallible. But God is not. He is without sin, so you can totally trust Him with all of your heart, and you will never, ever, be disappointed in Him.

Life's terrible circumstances may shake you to the core, but if you catch a glimpse of God's incredible integrity as well as His ability to keep His word, and therefore you trust Him, your faith will only grow through life's lion's den experiences. His promises are immutable. They are a solid rock. See Matthew 7:24–25 for details.

The God described by the Bible is omnipotent and can prevent anything. The God described in the Bible is claimed to be good. Now if I had the power to prevent a little girl from being raped, I would. The free will of the rapist would mean nothing at all to me. Anyone who placed the free will of the rapist over the safety of the little girl is evil. If someone stood by and watched the girl be raped and did nothing they would be as bad as the rapist. Your God is said to sit by and watch endless harm that could be prevented like some sick and cowardly voyeur. I would call such a creature evil, so why would I worship it, even if it were real?

You have touched on a very important point with the rape of a little girl. If God was good, it makes sense to think that He should immediately step in and (let's say for argument's sake) strike a child-rapist with lightning. Would that be okay with you?

You seem very righteous about the rape of a child. How about the rape and murder of an adult? How do you feel about hatred for someone? Or the desire they may have to rape a woman? How about lust in general? Envy? Fornication (sex outside of marriage)? Adultery? Greed? Rebellion? Ingratitude? Blasphemy? No doubt your call for immediate retribution stops at rape and murder because you don't see many of the above as being evil. God does. His standard of righteousness in infinitely higher than ours. Evil doesn't stop where you and I think it should, so if you are wanting Him to throw around bolts of lightning at that which He considers evil, you are talking about the entire human race, including yourself. In the eyes of God, you are no different from the rapist. So enjoy the grace He is giving you.

You will be pleased to know that the day is coming when He will bring His full wrath on your child rapist. The hymnwriter was right with his "He hath loosed the fateful lightning of His terrible swift sword."[68] Every human being (billions since the beginning of time) will stand before a holy God and be punished for their crimes against His law. So before you point your finger at others and ask why God doesn't punish them, you had better point it at yourself and make peace with Him before that day. Go through the Ten Commandments with a tender conscience, and if you have an honest heart you will see that you have a multitude of sins and dare not lift a holier-than-thou finger, point it at another, and call for the justice of God.

Wow, Ray, I have personally answered your versions of infinite regression, and "nothing creating everything" and corrected your pathetic misunderstanding of the second law of thermodynamics. . . . Not that I am claiming you are lying in this regard, I don't think so. You are simply expressing your ignorant opinions. However, if you had any intellectual honesty you would acknowledge that there are answers given to your supposed stumpers that you are unable to refute.

I am happy to acknowledge that answers have been given to explain the "nothing created everything" dilemma, but those answers are wrong. There's nothing to refute.

I have seen numbers of those who called themselves "atheists" change their minds and admit that they weren't atheists the moment they realized that they did believe that "something" created everything. That was because the alternative was ridiculous. That realization is the pin that pops the bubble of atheism. That's why I am staying with this, much to the annoyance of the faithful posters.

However, my consolation is that if they don't like me saying this, they are free to go elsewhere. Think about it. If every professing atheist leaves, this would no longer be "Atheist Central." The blog would dry up. I would be out of their lives forever. Or could it be that they get bored talking to those others who profess to be atheists?

So what do you believe: Creator or no creator? You could say that there is no such thing as "creation," which many atheists say, which is absurd. You could say, "I don't know." But if you do, you are not an atheist. You are agnostic. You could try to define "nothing" as being something, which is also ridiculous. One of your atheist friends said, "An atheist is someone who believes 'the something' is *not intelligent*, because cosmology, abiogenesis, and evolution show you don't need an intelligent designer to end up with a planet filled with life." Crazy talk. So you do have a dilemma.

Here's another atheist's attempt to distance himself from the essence of atheism: "Let's say I believe that something caused the universe to form. *Something* not *nothing*. However, I think that something was natural and not God. See, I am still an atheist because I don't believe in God, and yet at the same time I believe that something caused the universe." So he believes in a Creator as the cause of the universe. He's not an atheist.

But to think that you've somehow trumped your atheist "enemies" by denouncing them for not acknowledging a Supreme Being who, by your admission, is not the loving God you proclaim he is, is a reverse double bluff.

I don't consider you as enemies. I would like to see every atheist as my friend. Neither do I consider myself as being better than you, although I do see myself as being infinitely better off in the light of eternity. If I could score one point with those who profess atheism, it's to convince them that the god they don't believe in doesn't exist. Each of us, until we are "regenerated" by the Holy Spirit, has our "understanding darkened." We are, as Einstein said, like a little child in a massive library. I would add "an illiterate" little child. We are incapable of understanding, and so like Job (see Job 38:2) our words are without knowledge.

When an atheist talks of God as being a God of love, I can understand the impossibility of reconciling His harsh judgments with His professed love. How could He kill humanity through the Noahic Flood or mercilessly kill all the Canaanites, and still be called "loving"? It makes no sense.

The answer is simple. It is because He is also "just" and "holy." To help us understand this, we must take a moment to do something that is unpleasant. Think objectively about your sins. Be blatantly honest. Don't try to justify yourself. Go through the commandments one by one and ask if you are guilty of lying, stealing, blasphemy, lust, fornication, ingratitude, failure to love others as much as you love yourself, and of course the big one — failing to love God with all of your heart, mind, soul, and strength? Then ask how you would do if God lost patience and judged you right now by that perfect law, and you have to come to the conclusion that He hasn't dealt with you according to your sins. He hasn't treated you as He treated the Noahic generation or the Canaanites.

If we remove God's moral law (the Ten Commandments) from the equation, this "God of love" and the harsh judgments we read in the Bible are diametrically opposed. But when the Law enters and we understand that He is both just and holy and loving and merciful, then we begin to get a right image of the God we must face.

This has never been so clearly illustrated as at the Cross. There we see an evident display of God's wrath against sin as the Lamb of

God suffered for the sin of the world. But we also see an evident and amazing display of the love and mercy of God, when we understand that He suffered in Christ so that our case could be dismissed (see Romans 5:8). Still, what I am saying is just words, and all the talk in the world cannot help you in this case. You need to "taste" what I am saying, because you are dying for want of the Bread of Life (see John 6:35). Every minute of every day is drawing you closer to breathing your last. The minute that you "taste and see that the LORD is good," the life of God will enter your dying body, and the argument about His existence and the Savior He provided will be over. You will know the truth and the truth will make you free (see John 8:31–32).

When you claim that atheists believe "nothing created everything," and that it is pitifully dishonest and stupid to believe that, you're making a complete and utter fool of yourself when the next sentence out of your mustachio'd mouth is that "nothing created the creator who created everything," and that there's absolutely nothing wrong whatsoever with believing that. How is that even different?

Good question. It's different in that it is the dimension of "time" that demands a beginning. If time didn't exist there would be no beginning. Time is God's creation and He dwells outside of its limits. He is eternal. Creation (the universe) dwells within the element of time (is temporal) and therefore had to have a beginning. It's very simple.

One of the central arguments of The God Delusion *by Dawkins is this . . . "the designer hypothesis immediately raises the larger problem of who designed the designer?"*[69]

You will find a brilliant response and refutation to this argument by William Lane Craig. I thought I would share Craig's response with those who have briefly alluded to Dawkins' reasoning in their respective posts. Craig succinctly expresses the following:

> Dawkins' claim here is that one is not justified in inferring design as the best explanation of the complex order of the universe because then a new problem arises: who designed the designer?
>
> This rejoinder is flawed on at least two counts. First, in order to recognize an explanation as the best, one needn't have an explanation of the explanation. This is an elementary point concerning inference to the best explanation as practiced in the philosophy of science. If archaeologists digging in the earth were to discover things looking like arrowheads and hatchet heads and pottery shards, they would be justified in inferring that these artifacts are not the chance result of sedimentation and metamorphosis, but products of some unknown group of people, even though they had no explanation of who these people were or where they came from. Similarly, if astronauts were to come upon a pile of machinery on the back side of the moon, they would be justified in inferring that it was the product of intelligent, extra-terrestrial agents, even if they had no idea whatsoever who these extra-terrestrial agents were or how they got there. In order to recognize an explanation as the best, one needn't be able to explain the explanation. In fact, so requiring would lead to an infinite regress of explanations, so that nothing could ever be explained and science would be destroyed. So in the case at hand, in order to recognize that intelligent design is the best explanation of the appearance of design in the universe, one needn't be able to explain the designer.[70]

My purpose for being here (and I can only speak for myself and not the other unbelievers here) is to stand up for reason and especially to try to dissuade anyone from spreading the myth of creationism, especially in public schools.

This is censorship at its worst. Those who are anti-knowledge see themselves as the intellectual saviors of poor dumb college students, who don't have the ability to think for themselves. These are the book burners, who do what they do for the good of society. Their society. And they do what they do in the name of "reason" and "science," when their atheistic belief is completely unreasonable and absolutely unscientific.

The atheist has no basis to say *reason* exists. What is the mass of logic? It has none. It is immaterial. Oh, no! Atheists say there is no immaterial because God may be there. We can use logic because we are made in the image of the logical God.

If you think atheism is scientific and reasonable, let me ask you some questions. Do you believe that nothing created everything? If you do, that's not only unscientific, it's unreasonable. This is because your "nothing" isn't nothing. It is something because it had the amazing ability to create everything. So do you then believe that something created everything, although you are not sure what that something was? That's reasonable.

Keeping in mind that the most intelligent of human beings can't create a grain of sand from nothing, do you think that that "something" that made everything was intelligent? It obviously is; and if you do believe the "force" that made the flowers, the birds, the trees, the human eye, and the sun, the moon, and the stars was intelligent, you then believe that there was an intelligent designer. You have just become an unscientific knuckle-dragger in the narrow-minded eyes of our learning institutions that embrace Darwinism.

But you are not alone if you believe in God. Many of our greatest scientists believed in the existence of a Creator: Galileo, Newton, Nicholas Copernicus, Francis Bacon, Michael Faraday, Louis Pasteur, and Kepler, just to name a few. Einstein (a theist who didn't believe in a personal God) rightly said, "Science without religion is lame; religion without science is blind."[71] He also said, "In view of such harmony in the cosmos which I, with my limited human mind, am able to recognize, there are yet people who say there is no God. But what really makes me angry is that they quote me for the support of such views."[72]

The incredible harmony in creation proves beyond a doubt to any *thinking* mind that there is a Creator . . . don't you think?

> *When I contrasted having absolute assurance of something with the word "probably," an atheist (Richard) replied, "All planes and elevators are probably safe. Accidents do happen. All knowledge is probable. . . . So the use of probably simply means the person is not as arrogant to assume he/she has absolute knowledge. Anybody who claims to have absolute knowledge is a liar.*

However (using his own standards of judgment), this man must be a liar, because he made a number of absolute statements in his reply. He said that "all" planes and elevators are probably safe. That means that he has absolute knowledge of all planes and elevators. There's not one plane or elevator in this entire universe with which he isn't perfectly familiar.

Then he does the same thing with his "all" knowledge. To say "all knowledge is probable," he must *have* all knowledge to know that it's probable. So he humbly claims omniscience. He thinks that he is God. Then he boasts of his humility (he's not arrogant like those who use absolute statements) and says, "Anyone who claims to have absolute knowledge is a liar" . . . which is an absolute statement.

Richard Dawkins shows the difference between the belief of the atheist and the experiential knowledge of the Christian with his "There is probably no God." The Christian knows God, while the professing atheist doesn't. He is an "atheist" — *a* ("without") *theist* ("God"). He is without God.

> *I knew the Lord. I walked in obedience and trust. I went to church. I read the Bible. I prayed. . . . I was jolted out of that by reading rationalist and atheist arguments. See, I've got a rational, skeptical mind.*

Are you skeptical about rationality? You may think that you have a rational mind, but it wasn't rational enough to see the trap that I set for you. You weren't clever enough to step around it like your atheist friends. Here is that "trap": As a professing atheist, you only have two alternatives when it comes to your Christian experience of knowing God. You could say that you "thought" you knew the Lord, but you didn't because He's not real. So that means that you were never a Christian. You *didn't* know Him. You faked it.

My friend Dan Barker faked it for 19 years. Judas only lasted for three, but Dan fooled himself and others for almost two decades.[73] Amazing. Some hypocrites fall away from the faith. Most don't. They will remain in the midst of God's people and will be sorted out on Judgment Day (Matthew 7:21–22).

The second alternative is to say that you knew the Lord. That's what you said of your experience. *You knew Him.* Therefore you are not an atheist because your admittance of "I knew the Lord" is an admission that God is a reality. That also means that atheism itself is a fallacy.

So do you want to backtrack? Was God real in your experience, or were you deceived? If you were deceived, then you have a propensity of gullibility and you need to rethink what you say you now don't believe. With such a weakness, you can't be sure of anything.

If I wasn't a Christian and watched secular television, I don't think I would be an atheist, but I certainly would be anti-religious. Common sense would have steered me in that direction. I don't know how many times I have seen the secular media devote TV news time to a knot in a tree that looks like the face of Jesus, or a pancake that looks like Mary. Recently the media devoted about five minutes of the news hour to a religious woman who found a stain in one of her cooking pots that looked like Mary. Well, she thought it did. She took it as a word from God about something she was wanting and passed it on to a friend to bring her friend good luck.

What kind of low-IQ demographic do the media aim at? Then again, they may broadcast stuff like this because they know that many of us are the people who believe the Bible (talking snakes, etc.), and so we too will see Mary in a pot.

I pulled a tissue out of a container some time ago and saw some instant origami. I even took a photo of it. I wasn't sure who it was supposed to be. It could have been Mary. It sure looked like her. If a ten-year-old toasted cheese sandwich that looked like the virgin Mary can be sold on eBay for $28,000, I'm sure I could have gotten half that much. Too bad I had a cold that day. . . .

Ray, could you explain to me what it means to "know the Lord"? I often hear you ask "ex-Christians" (in quotes for your benefit) if they "knew the Lord." I would like to better understand your relationship with the Lord. How do you communicate with Him? How does He communicate back? In what way can one know that they know the Lord in the same manner as you?

This is a great question. Let me first explain why I use the wording "know the Lord." This is the biblical definition of a Christian. It is used many times in Scripture, but it is particularly used in reference to the gospel, in Jeremiah 31:34:

> No more shall every man teach his neighbor, and every man his brother, saying, "Know the LORD," for they all shall know Me, from the least of them to the greatest of them, says the LORD. For I will forgive their iniquity, and their sin I will remember no more.

It is because Jesus took our sin upon Himself that we can be forgiven. That means instead of being separated from God (have no real consciousness of His presence or reality), we can have fellowship with Him. Jesus said, "And this is eternal life, that they may know You, the only true God, and Jesus Christ whom You have sent" (John 17:3).

I often say that there's no such thing as an atheist who is an "ex-Christian." This is because there are only two alternatives that the "ex-Christian" can choose. If he knew the Lord, then "the Lord" exists and there is therefore no such thing as atheism. Or he simply "thought he knew the Lord," then he didn't, and was therefore a false convert, a hypocrite (1 John 2:19). Some in this category fall away from the faith, but many stay within the Church as "goats" among the sheep and will be sorted out on Judgment Day. Notice Scripture's wording in reference to that Day:

> Not everyone who says to Me, "Lord, Lord," shall enter the kingdom of heaven, but he who does the will of My Father in heaven. Many will say to Me in that day, "Lord, Lord, have we not prophesied in Your name, cast out demons in Your name, and done many wonders in

Your name?" And then I will declare to them, "*I never knew you*; depart from Me, you who practice lawlessness!" (Matthew 7:21–24, italics added).

False converts don't "know the Lord." He "never knew" them. There was no intimate relationship with them because they were still in their sins (playing the hypocrite).

Now to the essence of your question: What does it mean to know the Lord? Probably the best way I could relate it to you would be to say that it is very similar to me knowing my wife. We are best friends. She is forever in my thoughts. At the moment we are in different locations — I am at my home office, and she is at our ministry. Our different locations don't change the fact of our relationship. I still know her, love her, and trust her implicitly.

The moment I repented and put my trust in Jesus, I began a relationship with God that is more real than my relationship with my wife. It has the same feelings, but it's not contingent upon those feelings, but rather on trust (as are all relationships). Even though I don't "see" God, as with the relationship with my wife even though we are apart, I still have a relationship with God. The Bible puts it this way:

> Without having seen Him, you love Him; though you do not [even] now see Him, you believe in Him and exult and thrill with inexpressible and glorious (triumphant, heavenly) joy. [At the same time] you receive the result (outcome, consummation) of your faith, the salvation of your souls (1 Peter:7–9; AMP).

How do I talk to God? The same way everyone else does. Most nights I get up to pray (around midnight — something I have done since 1982). How does He talk to me? Through the Bible. It's a "lamp to my feet and a light to my path" (Psalm 119:105). I have read the Bible every day without fail since my conversion in 1972. I communicate with Him through prayer, and He speaks to me through His Word.

Your final question was, "In what way can one know that they know the Lord in the same manner as you?" Simply humble yourself and take a look at the Ten Commandments with a tender conscience — have you lied, stolen, blasphemed, or looked with lust (adultery of the heart) — and judge yourself: guilty or innocent? Heaven or Hell? Then look to the Cross — God in the person of Jesus Christ taking your punishment upon Himself — paying the fine so that you could leave the courtroom. Through His death and Resurrection, you can have everlasting life. If you will repent (something the hypocrite fails to do) and trust the Savior, you will come to know the Lord. (See John 14:21 for details.)

> *If something as simple as matter requires a creator, why doesn't something as complex as God? If something as complex as God doesn't require a creator, why does something as simple as matter? The Hawker Hurricane.*

For those who don't know, the Hawker Hurricane was a British single-seat fighter aircraft that was designed and predominantly built by Hawker Aircraft Ltd. Presumably the person who said the above knows that, and he considers himself to be a real fighter.

However, his quote doesn't fly. Not in the slightest. It's such a thoughtless statement, I'm surprised that another person would bother to quote him.

The fact of the matter is that matter is not simple. It's unspeakably complex. Matter is the "stuff" of which creation is made, and it's so complex that with all our modern technology we don't know how to make it. Not even an atom of it. We can *reorganize* existing matter, but we can't create. Only God can do that.

Then again, I must remember that I'm dealing with people who are so unthinking that they could think that Hawker Aircraft Ltd. didn't (and doesn't) exist, and that the British single-seater just happened by itself. To them, truth about matter doesn't matter. Nothing did it.

Ray, are you suggesting that the universe works in such a way that we'd expect if there was no God?

Definitely not. It works the way God designed it, barring effects from the Fall at a universal level. We should come to Christ knowing that He will give us everlasting life the moment we repent and trust the Savior, but that we will still come under the same storms as the unsaved. When it rains, Christians get wet. Lightning falls on the just and the unjust. That's just the way it is since the Curse in Genesis 3. Christians get disease, feel pain, have financial problems, and shake when the earth quakes.

To say (because of these things) that there is no God is to fail to use our God-given brain. The smallest part of creation is adequate evidence for a thinking mind that there's a Creator. So-called "primitive" natives right up to the intellect of Einstein know that.

Then again, let me know when you have figured out how to make both male and female living birds from nothing, ones that can reproduce after their kind. Then once you have figured it out, do it. From nothing. Perhaps then we could revisit the issue.

Fantastic post, Ray, one of your best in a long time. You have really done a great job of showing how little respect you actually have for atheists. Please keep it up, these posts are just wonderful and do an amazing job of turning people away from your brand of theism. . . . Oh, I'm an atheist, by the way, in case you were unsure.

You are partly correct. I respect atheists because they are human beings, but I have no "respect" at all for atheism. What else should you expect from me? Remember what I believe — I am 100 percent convinced that (what you call) your "lack of belief" will bring you unspeakable pain. I therefore will do everything I can to try to warn you that what you are trusting in is utterly foolish. I know (with 100 percent conviction) that the moment an atheist dies he (or she) will cry, "Oh, no! There *is* a God, and I am a wicked sinner who has violated His perfect law!" I am horrified at that happening to anyone.

Again, I'm utterly convinced that Hell is a reality and it is the destination for those who are guilty before God (Luke 12:5). Yet He offers a complete reprieve. Your case can be dismissed because of the Cross. God can allow you to live forever, if you will repent and trust the Savior. And you want me to respect the fact that you laugh at His mercy. It would be easier to respect a child who thinks it's funny to play with a lit stick of dynamite.

Tell me, how would you react if someone you cared about was trusting his life to a faulty parachute? As he stands 10,000 feet above an unforgiving earth, wouldn't you reason with him about the foolishness of what he is doing? And if he laughed at you, mocked you, and even hated you, wouldn't you still plead with him? Of course you would, unless you are an uncaring person. Well, I'm not. I care even to tell you the truth.

Connect with Ray Comfort

twitter.com/RayComfort
facebook.com/official.Ray.Comfort
youtube.com/thewayofthemaster

Follow this link to read Ray Comfort's daily blogs to atheists at "Atheist Central":
raycomfortfood.blogspot.com

You can also visit Ray's website, livingwaters.com

Ray co-hosts *The Way of the Master* television program with Kirk Cameron. Visit **wayofthemaster.com** to watch episodes of the show or find a station near you.

Connect with the Publisher:

twitter.com/masterbooks4u
facebook.com/masterbooks
join us at creationconversations.com

Appendix 1

In 2010 the news media revealed that according to professor Stephen Hawking, God didn't create the universe. Instead, nothing created everything. In an extract from his book *The Grand Design* the professor said:

> Because there is a law such as gravity, the Universe can and will create itself from nothing. Spontaneous creation is the reason there is something rather than nothing, why the Universe exists, why we exist.[74]

It is embarrassingly unscientific to speak of anything creating itself from nothing. Common sense says that if something possessed the ability to create itself from nothing, then that something wasn't nothing, it was something — a very intelligent creative power of some sort.

Stephen Hawking violated the unspoken rules of atheism. He wasn't supposed to use words like "create" or even "made." They necessitate a Creator and a Maker. Neither are you supposed to let out that the essence of atheism is to believe that nothing created everything, because it's unthinking. It confirms the title of one of my books — *You Can Lead an Atheist to Evidence, but You Can't Make Him Think*. Nor should an atheist speak of gravity as being a "law," because that also denotes the axiom of a Law-giver. Laws don't happen by themselves. But look at how careless the professor was with his: "The Big Bang was the result of the inevitable laws of physics and did not need God to spark the creation of the Universe."[75]

It seems that Professor Hawking has changed his mind about the need for God. Back in 1988, in his book *A Brief History of Time,* he said, "If we discover a complete theory . . . it would be the ultimate triumph of human reason — for then we should know the mind of God."[76]

Einstein said that he wanted to know the mind of God. Both men could have easily found the mind of God and through it have seen how we were created: "In the beginning, God created the heavens and the earth," something of which we were reminded when the astronauts on the first manned mission to the moon read from Genesis chapter 1. We need to read it again.

Quotes from Famous Atheists Who Went to Meet Their Maker

I have encountered a few creationists and because they were usually nice, intelligent people, I have been unable to decide whether they were really mad, or only pretending to be mad. If I was a religious person, I would consider creationism nothing less than blasphemy. Do its adherents imagine that God is a cosmic hoaxer who has created that whole vast fossil record for the sole purpose of misleading mankind?[77] — Arthur C. Clarke

No god ever gave any man anything, nor answered any prayer, nor ever will. . . . The purpose of human life is *not* to prepare yourself for death. The purpose of human life is to live, free of fears, guilt, anxieties, and feelings of personal inadequacy.[78] — Madalyn Murray O'Hair

Religion has actually convinced people that there's an invisible man living in the sky who watches everything you do, every minute of every day. And the invisible man has a special list of ten things he does not want you to do. And if you do any of these ten things, he has a special place, full of fire and smoke and burning and torture and anguish, where he will send you to live and suffer and burn and choke and scream and cry forever and ever 'til the end of time![79] — George Carlin

My philosophy is as simple as ever. I love smoking, drinking . . . reading and writing (not arithmetic). I have a selfless absorption in the well-being and achievements of Noel Coward. . . . In spite of my unregenerate spiritual attitude, I am jolly kind to everybody and still attentive and devoted to my dear old Mother.[80] — Noel Coward

One must choose between God and Man, and all "radicals" and "progressives," from the mildest liberal to the most extreme anarchist, have in effect chosen Man.[81] — George Orwell

If somebody is really sick, I don't pray to God, I look for the best doctor in town.[82] — Richard Rodgers

The whole conception of a God is a conception derived from the ancient oriental despotisms. It is a conception quite unworthy of free men. When you hear people in church debasing themselves and saying that they are miserable sinners, and all the rest of it, it seems contemptible and not worthy of self-respecting human beings. We ought to stand up and look the world frankly in the face.[83] — Bertrand Russell

You know, they are fooling us, there is no God. . . . All this talk about God is sheer nonsense.[84] — Joseph Stalin

I would love to believe that when I die I will live again, that some thinking, feeling, remembering part of me will continue. But much as I want to believe that, and despite the ancient and worldwide cultural traditions that assert an afterlife, I know of nothing to suggest that it is more than wishful thinking.[85] — Carl Sagan

That men do not learn very much from the lessons of history is the most important of all the lessons of history.[86] — Aldous Huxley

Appendix 2

NOTE: The following information is in response to a YouTube video titled "10 questions that every intelligent Christian must answer," which had almost six million views. Its main question was "Why won't God heal amputees?"

It's a standard practice of a manipulator to first flatter his hearers, then to phrase his question so that it contains the answer he wants — "You're an intelligent lad, so answer me 'Yes' or 'No.' Do you still beat your mother?"

Question One: So let's play this manipulative game for a moment as we address the first question: "Why won't God heal amputees?" If you are an intelligent person, also ask yourself this question: "Why won't God put money in the bank accounts of the poor? It has never happened; therefore, God doesn't exist." Here's another one: "Why is it that God never grows new hair on bald men's heads? All balding men pray for new hair, and you know that He completely ignores them. Therefore, God doesn't exist." Here's some more: "Can God make a rock that is too heavy for Him to lift?" or "Can He make a square circle?" These are powerful intellectual arguments that prove to the intelligent, thinking, clever, logical, rational, and educated mind that God doesn't exist. If, however, after using such critical-thinking skills you conclude that He doesn't exist, you are left with the scientific impossibility of having the inept belief that nothing created everything. There's no alternative for a thinking person.

Question Two: "Why are there so many starving people in our world?" Let's take this a little further. Why do so many children and adults get cancer, die of other terrible diseases, and drown in water? Why are so many burned to death in fire, get crushed by earthquakes, die in tornadoes and hurricanes, are killed by animals, and even murdered by their own parents? So the question becomes, "If God existed and is good and loving, He would do something about these terrible things." The Book of Genesis gives a perfectly rational explanation as to why all these things happen (but that's in the Bible and it is therefore inadmissible, for a thinking person). The conclusion is that God doesn't do anything to stop evil or suffering, therefore He doesn't exist. Nothing created everything.

Question Three: "Why does God demand the death of so many innocent people in the Bible?" Answer: He doesn't demand the death of any innocent people. He demands the death of guilty people, not only in the Bible, but also on this whole sinful earth. We will all experience the reality of death, because we are all guilty of violating His moral Law (see Romans 6:23). We are also told (among other things) that "God demands that we kill disobedient teenagers." This is not true. Why would anyone in today's society instigate the 3,000 year-old injunctions of Hebrew civil law? God demands no such thing of any of us.

Question Four: "Why does the Bible contain so much anti-scientific nonsense?" Answer: God supernaturally created all things, and He therefore has the ability to suspend natural law. He parts seas, walks on water, prepares the belly of whales, floods the earth (for which there is ample empirical evidence),[87] and raises the dead. With God, nothing is impossible.

Question Five: "Why is God such a huge proponent of slavery in the Bible?" We tend to look at slavery through the eyes of the cruel American slave trade, where races of people were kidnapped and sold for slaves. Kidnapping was a crime that God consider to be so serious, it was punishable by death (see Exodus 21:16). Biblical "slavery" (a bond-servant) wasn't kidnapping, and it wasn't determined by skin color. Those who were in debt paid off their debt through becoming a bond servant (see Leviticus 25:39). After six years, the servant was given his freedom (see Deuteronomy 15:12). However, rather than have their freedom, some chose to stay as bondservants because Hebrew law not only provided for them, it legally protected them. For example, if a slave was mistreated and died at the hands of his master, the master was to be put to death himself (see Exodus 21:20–21). The Law of Moses did allow the use of enemy slave labor, as did America with German soldiers captured during World War II.[88] Not every ordinance in "the Law of Moses" should be considered to be God's will, as in the case of divorce (see Matthew 19:7–8).

Question Six: "Why do bad things happen to good people?" Answer: Bad things don't happen to good people. This is because there are no "good" people according to the Bible (see Psalm 14:1–3). God's definition of a "good" person is someone who is morally perfect — in thought, word, and in deed. Only God is good. A more relevant question would be, "Why do good things happen to bad people?" The answer is that God has lavished His kindness upon us, despite our many sins.

Question Seven: "Why didn't any of Jesus' miracles in the Bible leave any evidence?" What sort of "evidence" should we expect to see from His walking on water, or the feeding of the 5,000, or the raising of the dead — wet feet, bread crumbs or fish bones, or returned undertakers' checks? There is of course the real evidence of eyewitness testimony (but that's in the Bible, and it is therefore inadmissible).

Question Eight: "How do we explain the fact that Jesus has never appeared to you?" These questions are getting even weaker, and a little weird.

Question Nine: "Why would Jesus want you to eat His body and drink His blood?" Answer: He doesn't. When the Bible says "And as they were eating, Jesus took bread, blessed and broke it, and gave it to the disciples and said, 'Take, eat; this is My body' " (Matthew 26:26). He was physically with His disciples, so any intelligent, educated, rational person would know that His words were not "disgusting, cannibalistic satanic ritual," but were symbolic. The wine and the bread were symbols (metaphors) of His blood and His body.

Question Ten: "Why do Christians get divorced at the same rate as non-Christians?" Answer: They don't. Skeptics are continually saying that "the Church is filled with hypocrites," and this is one proof that it is. A hypocrite is a pretending (fake) Christian. The Bible calls them "goats" that mix among the "sheep," and God warns that He will sort them out on Judgment Day (by the way, divorce is allowed for Christians, if a spouse commits adultery — see Matthew 19:9).

The presupposition for most of these ten questions is that if God was good, He would heal amputees, feed the starving, stop bad things from happening, not be a proponent of slavery, and do miracles when we tell Him to do them. Then the conclusion is that because He doesn't stop them (or obey us by performing miracles), He therefore doesn't exist. However, there is one conclusion to which intelligent people should arrive when it comes to God being good. If He is truly good, He must (like a good judge) see to it that ultimate justice is carried out. He must make sure that murderers, rapists, thieves, liars, adulterers, fornicators, blasphemers, etc., are punished. Judgment Day makes sense to an intelligent educated person, if God is good.

In conclusion, let me show you something remarkable. Some people believe that God is imaginary. They imagine that He doesn't exist, and then imagine that nothing therefore created everything. Then they say to themselves, *That makes complete sense. All scientific evidence supports this conclusion.* That's called "delusionary." As the Bible points out, such people profess to be wise, but they are fools (see Romans 1:20–22). Rather than following such delusionary thought, it would be wise to use our God-given brain to say, "I am offered everlasting life through the gospel. An intelligent person would at least look into it." Please take the time to do that — rather than listen to fools. See: NeedGod.com

Endnotes

1. Eyler Robert Coates Sr., compiler and editor, *Thomas Jefferson on Politics & Government,* "To Mrs. M. Harrison Smith," 1816. Memorial Edition, 15:60, http://etext.virginia.edu/jefferson/quotations/jeff1650.htm.

2. Statement to German anti-Nazi diplomat and author Prince Hubertus zu Lowenstein around 1941, as quoted in his book *Towards the Further Shore: An Autobiography* (London: Gollancz, 1968).

3. Albert Paine, *Mark Twain's Notebook* (Hesperides Press, 2006).

4. Albert Henry Smyth, editor, *The Writings of Benjamin Franklin* (New York: Haskell House Publishers, 1970), Vol. ii., p. 2.

5. Charles Darwin, *The Autobiography of Charles Darwin* (Cambridge, UK: Icon Books, Ltd., 2003), p. 149.

6. Roy P. Basler and Christian O. Basler, editors, *The Collected Works of Abraham Lincoln* (New Brunswick, NJ: Rutgers University Press, 1990), VII:334.

7. http://machineslikeus.com/news/why-carl-sagan-considered-good-atheist.

8. Jeffrey Meyers, *Hemingway: A Biography* (London: Macmillan, 1985), p. 560.

9. Harry Gilroy, "Widow Believes Hemingway Committed Suicide," *New York Times* (August 23, 1966).

10. http://scienceblogs.com/pharyngula/2008/07/an_inspirational_poster. php.

11. http://scienceblogs.com/pharyngula/2008/07/an_inspirational_poster. php.

12. Sir David Brewster, *Memoirs of the Life, Writings and Discoveries of Sir Isaac Newton,* "A Short Scheme of the True Religion" (Edinburgh: Thomas Constable and Co., 1850).

13. LiveScience Staff, "Swearing Makes Pain More Tolerable," www.livescience. com/health/090712-swearing-pain.html.

14. Herman Friedrich Graebe, testimony given at Nuremberg trials, http:// www.absoluteastronomy.com/topics/Hermann_Friedrich_Graebe.

15. William Shakespeare, *Macbeth*, act 5, scene 1, lines 26–40.

16. www.newsweek.com/id/109373.

17. Rit Nosotro, 2003, www.hyperhistory.net/apwh/bios/b4edisont.htm.

18. Ibid.

19. Robert L. Herrmann, *God, Science, and Humility: Ten Scientists Consider Humility Theology,* "The Limits of Knowledge and the Hope for Progress," by Francisco J. Ayala (Philadelphia, PA: Templeton Foundation Press, 2000), p. 132.

20. Laurence Moran, "What Is Evolution?" www.talkorigins.org/faqs/evolution-definition.html.

21. Here is the response from the original skeptic: "Ray, looking over those verses, I find that most of them make perfect, obvious sense if you render *sheol* as 'the grave' rather than 'Hell.' . . . I stand by my contention that post-death punishment is a concept absent from most of the Old Testament." My reply: "There are *many* words you can substitute for the word 'Hell' if you want to, and each verse still makes perfect sense. However, all you are doing is twisting Scripture 'to your own destruction' and to the destruction of those who believe you. I notice that you backed down by using the word 'most' twice. Why not rather apologize and say that you were wrong, humbling though it is? This is *such* an important issue. Think of the implications. . . ."

22. "At Calvary," by William R. Newell and Daniel B. Towner, 1895.

23. Richard Dawkins, *The God Delusion* (Boston, MA: Houghton Mifflin, 2006), p. 31.

24. Charles Darwin, *The Origin of Species* (London: J. Murray, 1859), chapter 6, p. 184.

25. Ibid., chapter 6.

26. Duke University Medical Center, "The Human Appendix: A Biological 'Remnant' No More," *ScienceDaily* (August 21, 2009), www.sciencedaily.com/releases/2009/08/090820175901.htm.

27. http://en.wikipedia.org/wiki/Evolution_of_sexual_reproduction.

28. Richard Dawkins, *The Ancestor's Tale* (Boston, MA: Houghton Mifflin, 2004).

29. Richard Dawkins, *The Greatest Show on Earth: The Evidence for Evolution* (New York: Free Press, 2009) p. 8-9.

30. www.discoverymagazine.com/digger/d01dd/d0102dd.html.

31. Loren G. Martin, "What Is the Function of the Human Appendix?" *Scientific American* (October 21, 1999).

32. See T.E. Southard, "Third Molars and Incisor Crowding: When Removal Is Unwarranted," *Journal of the American Dental Association* 123(8):75–78) (1992).

33. Stephen Hawking, *Hadron, Hawking, Humanism & the Death of True*

Science (HD, updated), www.youtube.com/watch?v=zW5-aQonz3E.

34. Nilesh Parekh, "Potassium Deficiency: Effects of Low Potassium," *Buzzle,* www.buzzle.com/articles/potassium-deficiency-effects-of-low-potassium. html.

35. "Vitamins and Minerals: What Is Calcium?" *Essortment,* www.essortment. com/all/vitaminsmineral_rszw.htm.

36. "What Is Magnesium?" *Essortment,* www.essortment.com/all/whatismag-nesiu_rtca.htm.

37. "Phosphorous," *Internet Health Library,* www.internethealthlibrary.com/ DietandNutrition/Phosphorus.htm.

38. "Iron in Diet," *MedlinePlus,* www.nlm.nih.gov/medlineplus/ency/arti-cle/002422.htm.

39. "Manganese Poisoning, Manganism, Parkinsonism, Wilson's Disease, and Parkinson's Disease," www.manganese-wilsons-parkinsons-disease.com.

40. http://www.livescience.com/health/top10_missinglinks-1.html.

41. http://raycomfortfood.blogspot.com/2009/10/honest-atheist.html.

42. JoAnne Allen, "Schools Infested with Drugs: Teen Survey," http:// uk.reuters.com/article/idUKN1640311120070817.

43. Lawrence K. Altman, "Sex Infections Found in Quarter of Teenage Girls," *New York Times,* http://www.nytimes.com/2008/03/12/science/12std. html.

44. "Teen Suicide Prevention," *State Health Lawmakers' Digest,* Fall 2005, http://www.ncsl.org/default.aspx?tabid=14111.

45. John Cochran, "Failing Reports on U.S. Schools," *ABC World News,* April 26, 2008, http://abcnews.go.com/WN/story?id=4732319&page=1.

46. Kim A. Bard, "Are Humans the Only Primates That Cry?" *Scientific American,* May 8, 2006, http://www.scientificamerican.com/article. cfm?id=are-humans-the-only-prima.

47. http://nobelprize.org/nobel_prizes/medicine/laureates/1962/crick-lec-ture.html.

48. Richard Dawkins, *The Blind Watchmaker* (New York: Norton, 1986).

49. This was written in 1857 as Darwin worked toward the publication of his theory, and has been related to his memories of his time at university when an "Infidel home missionary tour" by the Reverend Robert Taylor warned Darwin of the dangers of dissent from church doctrine. While Taylor was subsequently nicknamed "the devil's chaplain," the term goes back further, and Geoffrey Chaucer has his Parson (in *Canterbury Tales*) say, "Flatereres been the develes chapelleyns, that syngen evere placebo" in a reference to

Placebo (at funeral); "Darwin's Child," profile by Simon Hattenstone, *The Guardian* (February 10, 2003). Also Adrian Desmond, *Huxley: From Devil's Disciple to Evolution's High Priest* (Reading, MA: Addison-Wesley, 1997), p. 228.

50. John Tooby, "The Greatest Englishman Since Newton," *New York Times,* October 6, 2002.

51. Ibid.

52. http://www.actionbioscience.org/evolution/futuyma.html.

53. http://www.guardian.co.uk/world/2003/feb/10/religion.scienceandnature.

54. Richard Weikart, *From Darwin to Hitler* (New York: Palgrave Macmillan, 2004), p. 186.

55. Richard Darwin Keynes, editor, *Charles Darwin's Beagle Diary* (Cambridge; New York: Cambridge University Press, 1988).

56. Francis Darwin, editor, *The Life and Letters of Charles Darwin,* Vol. 2 (McLean, VA: IndyPublishing, 2002).

57. "Race Remarks Get Nobel Winner in Trouble," Associated Press, 10/18/2007, www.msnbc.msn.com/id/21362732/.

58. Helen Nugent, "Black People 'Less Intelligent' Scientist Claims," *London Times* (October 17, 2007); www.timesonline.co.uk/tol/news/uk/article2677098.ece.

59. Charlotte Hunt-Grubbe, "The Elementary DNA of Dr. Watson," *London Sunday Times* (October 14, 2007); www.entertainment.timesonline.co.uk/tol/arts_and_entertainment/books/article2630748.ece.

60. Carl Sagan, *Cosmos* (New York: Random House, 1980).

61. Charles H. Spurgeon, *An All-round Ministry: Addresses to Ministers and Students* (Edinburgh, UK: Banner of Truth Trust, 1978).

62. "Thunderf00t" was the pseudonym of a well-known atheist who debated Ray Comfort on the subject of the existence of God.

63. www.youtube.com/watch?v=aecYCWBM8TI&feature=relate.

64. www.livingwaters.com.

65. "Former Christian Songwriter Dan Barker Now an Atheist," *Metro Silicon Valley,* October 3–9, 2002. http://metroactive.com/papers/metro/10.03.02/barker-0240.html. Barker received a degree in religion from Azusa Pacific University and became an ordained minister in 1975. In 1984 he announced to his friends that he was an atheist.

66. www.trueorigin.org/sex01.asp.

67. First Amendment, U.S. Constitution (italics added).

68. "The Battle Hymn of the Republic," by Julia Ward Howe.

69. Richard Dawkins, *The God Delusion* (Boston, MA: Houghton Mifflin, 2006), p. 157–158.

70. William Lane Craig, "What Do You Think of Richard Dawkins' Argument for Atheism in *The God Delusion?*" http://www.reasonablefaith.org/site/News2?page=NewsArticle&id=5493.

71. Albert Einstein, "Science, Philosophy and Religion: a Symposium," 1941, http://www.sacred-texts.com/aor/einstein/einsci.htm#TWO.

72. Statement to German anti-Nazi diplomat and author Prince Hubertus zu Lowenstein around 1941, as quoted in his book *Towards the Further Shore: An Autobiography* (London: Gollancz, 1968).

73. http://www2.ljworld.com/news/2004/nov/13/former_preacher_deconverts.

74. Stephen Hawking and Leonard Mlodinow, *The Grand Design* (New York: Bantam, 2010).

75. Ibid.

76. Stephen Hawking, *A Brief History of Time* (New York: Bantam, 1988), p. 193.

77. Arthur C. Clarke, "Presidents, Experts, and Asteroids," *Science,* vol. 280, no. 5369 (June 5, 1998): p. 1532–3].

78. Madalyn O'Hair, "Fundamentalism," address delivered on October 22, 1986, www.positiveatheism.org/writ/fund'ism.htm.

79. www.rense.com/general69/obj.htm.

80. www.criticalcompendium.com/the-letters-of-noel-coward-edited-by-barry-day/.

81. www.positiveatheism.org/hist/quotes/quote-o.htm.

82. Meryle Secrest, *Somewhere for Me: A Biography of Richard Rodgers* (New York: Knopf, 2001).

83. Bertrand Russell, "Why I Am Not a Christian," http://www.positiveatheism.org/hist/russell0.htm.

84. E. Yaroslavsky, *Landmarks in the Life of Stalin* (London: Lawrence & Wishart Ltd., 1942).

85. Carl Sagan, *Billions and Billions* (New York: Random House, 1997), p. 215.

86. www.age-of-the-sage.org/history/quotations/lessons_of_history.html.

87. http://www.unmaskingevolution.com/18-flood.htm.

88. http://mshistory.k12.ms.us/index.php?id=233.